P9-DVO-692

Gangs
in
Canada

Gangs
in
Canada

Jeff Pearce

QUAGMIRE
PRESS

The Publisher: Quagmire Press Ltd.
Website: www.quagmirepress.com

Library and Archives Canada Cataloguing in Publication

Pearce, Jeff, 1963–
   Gangs in Canada / Jeff Pearce.

Soft Cover: ISBN 978-1-926695-07-5
Hard Cover: ISBN 978-1-926695-10-5

1. Gangs—Canada. 2. Juvenile delinquents—Canada. 3. Gang prevention—Canada. 4. Juvenile delinquency—Canada—Prevention. I. Title.

HV6439.C3P42 2009   364.106'60971   C2009-905940-1

Project Director: Hank Boer
Project Editor: Nicholle Carrière
Cover Image: Photos.com
Author Photo: Courtesy of E. Thomas Canton

We gratefully acknowledge the support of the Alberta Foundation for the Arts for our publishing program.

COMMITTED TO THE DEVELOPMENT OF CULTURE AND THE ARTS

PC: 13

Contents

INTRODUCTION 9

Chapter 1: THE BATTLEFIELD IN PARADISE 16

Chapter 2: A WARRIOR'S RELIGION 34

Chapter 3: THE CONSTABLE..50

Chapter 4: THE NEW WILD WEST: CALGARY 67

Chapter 5: THE NEW WILD WEST: WINNIPEG 81

Chapter 6: "IT'S THE CHOICES OUR SONS MADE" 99

Chapter 7: "YOU DON'T DO THIS, THEN IT'S GOING
              TO HAPPEN TO YOU"...124

Chapter 8: GIRLS AND BOYS 136

Chapter 9: THE GRIM, THE GOOD AND THE GUNS........................... 145

Chapter 10: ROLLING BOILS AND SLOW SIMMERS 178

Chapter 11: THE SELF-CLEANING OVEN 191

Chapter 12: PATCHWORK: HOW THE HELLS ANGELS RULE 204

Chapter 13: THE WAY THE STORY'S TOLD..225

Chapter 14: COMPLAINTS AGAINST CULTURE: A PERSONAL VIEW ...237

Chapter 15: POSTSCRIPT: A CHANCE FOR A NORMAL LIFE 251

Dedication

Because this book focuses at times on mentors and those trying to have a positive influence on young people, it is for two people who made a difference in my life: Rusty Rischuk and Delle Bonneau.

It's also for my beloved daughter, Lily. This is how part of the world was when you were growing up, sweetheart. I hope we figure out how to fix it by the time you're older and might want to read this slim volume.

Acknowledgements

I would like to thank Nicholle Carrière for her painless editing skills and my publisher, as always, for infinite patience. I would also like to thank several individuals for giving generously of their time and without whose help this book would have been woefully incomplete: Mani Amar, Renu Bakshi, Gilles Benoit, Patti Bruneau, Kathy Buddle, Neil Castro, Blair Cosgrove, Kevin Daniels, Sharon Davis, Gordon Eiriksson, Lenni Folden-Su'a, Julie Gagnon, Rob Gordon, Rhyse Hanson, Len Isnor, Jas Kainth, Shinder Kirk, James Lathlin, Simon Malbogat, Duncan McCallum, Jessie McKay, Brian Palmeter, Mike Porteous, Mark Pugash, Heather Robertson, Jacques Robinette, Don Spicer, David Setter, Shane, Audette Shephard, Brody Smollet, Nichole Stewart, Garrett Swihart, Carla Turner, Jason van Rassel and Jacqui Wasacase.

The reader should understand that my conclusions and any factual errors are mine alone.

The pitch-black of the park was suddenly firefly alive with gunbursts and sparkler flame. Most of the shots were going wild, but occasionally I could hear a thrashing and a coughing in the trees. Blood seemed to be drenching me, not sweat....

Someone was lying under a tree, clutching his chest and "Hail Mary's" with bloody fingers and a swollen tongue.

Beside me, Fence rasped, "Now? Now I do it? Huh, now?"

I laid a hand down on his back to shut up.

Not yet.

Let's live a little longer...

—Harlan Ellison, describing an actual gang fight in Prospect Park, Brooklyn, in Memos From Purgatory

Introduction

G angs have always been with us. The Romans, both in Republican and Imperial times, tolerated and even indulged their adolescents running around in gangs. One gang was known to have broken into the home of a prostitute to rape her. Gangs frequently had the run of the streets, beating up strangers, sexually assaulting women and vandalizing shops. Imagine it, boys in woollen and cotton tunics, descending on your average innocent citizen in a toga, going about his business.

These weren't kids from broken homes and slums, either. "Come home for dinner as soon as possible," goes a letter quoted in one modern history of Roman private life, "for a gang of hot-headed youths from the best families is pillaging the city." As an adolescent, Nero ran with one and nearly became a gang-related homicide; a senator who fought back during an attack didn't recognize him and beat the hell out of him.

Gangs have always been with us.

When I mentioned I was writing this book to an old friend from high school back in Winnipeg, one who was living in Los Angeles, he sent me an email with the subject line "Memories" and quick, bullet-point-style anecdotes. He started with the grandfather of his wife "regaling me with stories of his old Jessie Street gang carrying guns, knives, etc. in River Heights back in the day.

"Gang fight between St. Vital and Fort Rouge/Fort Gary over squatting rights...carrying knives, planks with nails and chains to the fight. The cops breaking it all up.

"My mom facing down Vietnamese gang members in her Daniel Mac library, nursing a kid who was stabbed in the stacks.

"Visiting my brother in the ER after he'd literally had his head kicked in after he'd stupidly stopped to see what was going on late one night when he noticed a park bench being torched on his way home after a party.

"Comforting my sister after they found her boyfriend with a bullet in his head, in the trunk of his car, in the Vancouver Harbour after he'd flown from Winnipeg to talk to the Chinese manager in order to figure out where the cash was disappearing from his family's carpet business."

And this isn't the entire list. He didn't relate tales about the infamous Crips and Bloods from the city where he's been living more recently. He passed on incidents that happened in

Canada. More amazingly, this was all rattled off by a success-ful, nice guy in his 40s who has a beautiful, accomplished wife, lovely kids—a guy, who from what I can tell, lives a pretty middle-class existence. And gang life has touched him and his family over the course of two decades.

Gangs have *always* been with us.

The question is whether or not we allow them to follow us into the centuries ahead. It's an urgent question given that Statistics Canada says gang-related violence accounted for almost one in four homicides in the country in 2008.

Here in Canada, gangs run the gamut from the Indo-Canadians in Vancouver to Aboriginal gangs in Manitoba to racist thugs in Calgary to the notorious Hells Angels who fought a brutal and bloody war with their rivals in Québec. As we'll see, however, a "Punjabi gang" or a "Vietnamese gang" may not be totally Punjabi or Vietnamese at all. The shorthand is sometimes far from accurate. We're a multicul-tural country and, so it seems, is our crime. Gangs are multiplying in all shapes, sizes and ethnicities.

The scale of our gang problem is literally nationwide, and so its treatment in this book can't be exhaustive. Instead, it will zero in on key cities at the expense of others to show-case certain unique elements or problems. We will begin with Vancouver, because its situation combined with the Winter Olympics has earned it less-than-flattering interna-tional attention, and then we will move from west to east, hopefully confounding some expectations (if you thought

Toronto, our biggest city, had the biggest gang problem, think again). You can read these chapters as stand-alone segments, but just to let you know, like plot twists in a thriller without end, certain themes come back to haunt our cities in surprising ways. Every province is different, but they do have a few things in common.

The lines, in fact, blur between what is "gang-related" and what better fits under the heading of organized crime. Gangs can be loose associations or they can be relatively sophisticated in their methods and success, but generally speaking, we're talking about criminal groups that attract youth as members.

Another problem is that the chessboard keeps changing. The figures discussed in this slim little tome are living on borrowed time—many gang members mentioned in the narrative are likely to be sitting in a prison cell or lying in a pool of blood by the time this book hits the shelves. That's neither a prediction nor a threat—it's a statement of fact. Given enough time, as the philosophical narrator in the movie *Fight Club* would put it, their survival rate "will drop to zero."

Because the players keep changing, it would date the book badly and make it pointless to just summarize a series of high-profile cases or to profile key individuals. Yes, this book can't help but include some of that, but it struggles for a very different approach. It will look at some individuals, but also explore facets of gang activity as a collection of criminal institutions themselves. That is, after all, what they've become.

That raises a question that's on many people's minds: Why would anyone even want to belong to a gang? What motivates these young people to join? How do they get involved in this kind of life?

All of us who ask forget that even framing the questions says more about us than the gang members. If you've bought this book, chances are you come from a middle-class background or better and live a life in which you have always had choices. Yes, you might have divorced parents, you might have had personal setbacks in your life, but if you're reading this, odds are that you came from a relatively stable environment with reasonably good teachers, with a good education and work prospects. It would never occur to you to think of crime as a career path, would it? Go out and rob a store? Deal drugs? Beat the daylights out of somebody? We've been taught the potential consequences of such drastic behaviour, criminal behaviour, and we would never think of risking what we have.

But there's a surprise in store. As we'll discover, not all gang members come from broken homes. Or poor ones. Or from minority households.

To understand gangs, the pugnacious and controversial writer Harlan Ellison—who sees himself "as as a combination of Zorro and Jiminy Cricket"—actually joined one. Short in stature, he briefly belonged to the Barons in New

York City under an assumed name, running with them in the dangerous neighbourhood of Red Hook in Brooklyn in 1954. Now, I am too old and don't have either the stones or the insane fearlessness for an experiment like that.

What I did do is mine the online archives of newspaper articles and reports of talented journalists who have already done a lot of heavy lifting on this subject, from the work of Jason van Rassel of the *Calgary Herald* to documentary segments reported by Erin Collins and produced by Carla Turner for CBC Calgary. I spoke to former gang members and relatives of gang members. I found several cops willing to talk to me, but the cooperation of one force was so exceptional that the inclusion of names within my acknowledgements just won't cut it.

I have to offer a special thanks to Nichole Stewart, Garrett Swihart, Jas Kainth and Gordon Eiriksson of the Calgary Police Service, because I have never run across a more cooperative, candid and forthcoming group of police staff. These men and women *want* you to understand this problem, and they offered astonishing courtesies and were generous with their time so that you can wrap your head around it.

This book only makes sense if it presents not only a portrait of our gang problem across Canada, but also gives a voice to those fighting the war. There are relatively new initiatives and new approaches being taken, and we'll examine some of these. Talking to people across the country about gangs hasn't made me a gang expert by any stretch of the imagination, but towards the end of this book, I have "indulged" myself in two chapters in which I wanted to address certain concerns, ones on which I do feel qualified to comment—those on media and culture. As a journalist, I am concerned with how the media covers the gang issue, shaping our opinions. As a novelist and scriptwriter, I have a personal stake in how our popular culture might be shaping our young people.

In exploring the gang problem, we may discover it's not insurmountable. Our young people do not have to die or wind up behind bars. So this book humbly invites you to change your thinking. Then help change the thinking and behaviour of our children.

Chapter One

The Battlefield in Paradise

I n Vancouver, the situation deteriorated badly enough in 2009 that British periodicals rolled out sensationalistic headlines about the city's gangs and drug trade. On April 5 of that year, *The Independent* ran a piece for its Sunday edition titled, "From heaven to hell: 18 die as drugs war rages on streets of Vancouver." This was its thumbnail portrait in the first paragraph:

> *Once upon a very recent time, Vancouver had a clean, safe image. Nestled between a spectacular bay and snow-capped mountains, this Canadian city, which is twice the size of Birmingham, was described by* The Economist *as the most liveable in the world. Not any more. As it prepares to host the 2010 Winter Olympics, what it's got*

now is not cuddly, eco-friendly publicity, but blood-spattered streets littered with shell casings and corpses.

The article's author, Paul Rodgers, draws a lurid scene of Vancouver as a "battlefield" in which a *Who's Who* of top gangs, including the Hells Angels, Big Circle Boys, United Nations, Red Scorpions, Independent Soldiers and the 14K Triad, are all involved. "Guns—often machine guns—are fired almost daily." Canadian courts, he writes, are relatively lenient compared to American ones (which most law enforcement authorities agree is true, though the U.S. has more than two million people behind bars, so the legal system doesn't seem to be helping), and Vancouver's own mayor, Gregor Robertson, admits that police are losing the fight.

The article quotes an expert at Simon Fraser University, who suggests the problem only gets worse with police efforts to capture top crime organization leaders. "All you do is create vacancies as you put people in jail," claims Ehor Boyanowsky, an associate professor of criminology. "Suddenly there's an opportunity." Boyanowsky doesn't offer a solution for what to do instead, or at least *The Independent* didn't see fit to give him the space to outline his alternative.

The city's PR only got worse when *The Economist* asked for its May 28th issue, "British Columbia or Colombia?" The magazine noted that about 135 gangs are thought to be fighting over business worth an estimated $7 billion a year. "That they do so in broad daylight demonstrates the feckless response of the provincial government and police, despite reports dating back more than 30 years giving warning of the growth in organized crime."

But the attitudes, and the tactics, of authorities are changing, and things might be getting better.

~

Gangs weren't an overnight phenomenon in the Lower Mainland any more than they have been in Toronto or Montréal. The truth is, as police officers will admit all across the country, no one was paying them much attention.

With such a beautiful city in a mild climate sitting on the shores of the Pacific, one so close to the Asia-Pacific region, one would think it would be inevitable that it should become a major hub for drug trafficking and organized crime. Add to that British Columbia's rich forests and geography—perfect for growing marijuana, which is now the province's third largest industry, worth an estimated $8 billion a year. The crop is a de facto brand in its own right, known as "BC bud."

This is Business Number One for the gangs in British Columbia. This is what the fighting is all about here: controlling what comes in, as in cocaine, other drugs and illegal guns from the United States; making as much money as possible on the marijuana that goes out and often heads south; and making sure those who should pay, do. It is that simple. Rivalry here is over who takes the largest slice of the pie.

With such huge profits, the violence has ramped up. Besides drive-by shootings and murders at marijuana grow-ops, police in a raid on a "crack shack" in Prince George found a man tortured and shackled to a basement wall. And it wasn't the first time investigators had seen victims of gangs tortured, sometimes for as little as $100. Many of the victims aren't involved in criminal activity at all, they're simply innocent relatives. RCMP Constable Lesley Dix told the *Prince George Citizen* that this is the gang's way "with this extortion and kidnapping and beating, to show who is boss and to make them an example if they don't pay or if they steal from each other."

As fatalities rose into the double digits, Vancouver police acknowledged they were playing catch-up in a war that involved an alphabet soup of criminal organizations. "As police, we've always been told by media experts to never say or admit that there is a gang war," the force's chief, Jim Chu, told reporters. "Well, let's get serious. There is a gang war, and it's brutal."

To some degree, the mayhem has been misleading, suggesting it's a free-for-all, as if modern Huns or Visigoths were taking over the Lower Mainland at random. But police officials and experts have pointed out how gangs can have sophisticated, practically corporate structures and hierarchies.

Take, for example, the founder of the UN gang, Clayton Roueche, who pleaded guilty in the U.S. to conspiracy to smuggle pot and cocaine. He boasted about having ties to the underworld in Colombia. His gang spent $350,000 on two planes to bring in drugs, and officers who raided his home discovered a paper trail implicating him in close to $1 million in drug transactions.

His gang started with high school pals.

The name UN referred to the different ethnic backgrounds of the friends who all hung out together in Abottsford in the late 1990s. They quickly earned a reputation for solving their problems by drawing their guns, and they even made enemies for a while of the infamous Hells Angels, whom they fought in a notorious brawl in 2000 at the Animals nightclub right on their own home turf of Abbotsford. While the UN apparently has only about 100 members, the gang's indoctrination is supposed to be quite involved. Loyalty is sometimes taken to a grotesque degree. Consider a tombstone for gang member Evan Appell, who died from a drug overdose (the tombstone was actually used as an exhibit in Clayton Roueche's trial). The letters "UN" stand boldly larger than the name of the grave's occupant and includes the slogan "United Forever, Forever United" along with a note that he would be remembered by his "UN family."

Unfortunately for British Columbia, the UN gang has come a long way from high school.

So have the Red Scorpions, who got started in a youth detention centre in 2000 and who have been linked to some of the bloodiest violence that's grabbing headlines, including the murders of six people in a Surrey apartment block in 2007. Their members sport a tattoo of a medieval-style *R* and *S* on the wrist, neck or shoulder. Recruitment is sometimes simple and ruthless: they bring in new members by handing out free crack with a phone number that is staffed around the clock. But in June 2009, Sergeant Shinder Kirk of the province's Integrated Gang Task Force only put the central membership at 25.

And keep in mind that there are dozens of other gangs on the BC landscape. It's more useful at times to examine what they have in common than to pick over their individual habits and customs. Kirk has suggested, for instance, that many top gang leaders set up mid-level "puppet groups" that function as protective insulation. The gangs even use anonymous freelancers—individuals who have never had a run-in with the law—to smuggle drugs across the border. Kirk told the *Vancouver Sun*, "You can have a subcontractor who develops a smuggling route and was contracting his services out to individuals who have product." A delivery date is set, and orders are filled.

Some of the groups, says Kirk, have no hierarchy, while others have one that is very loose, "like a board of directors, if you will, with one chairperson." The experts say that gangs have borrowed organizational models from more advanced criminals, such as Colombian drug cartels, but they've added a spin of their own, "outsourcing" certain links in their business chain to various specialists. So while the violent rivalry among gangsters is getting a lot of attention, there's also a great deal of networking.

Still, even though affiliation for freelancers or puppet gangs doesn't have to be formal, it can also still prove deadly according to Abbotsford Police Chief Bob Rich. "Any young person out there now—because of the potential for retaliation and the confusion that exists over who is associated with who—is at risk if they are involved in the drug trade." The foot soldiers of the gang make the casualty list first.

"What we have seen are new rules of engagement for the gangsters," Vancouver Police Chief Jim Chu has pointed out. "They are now shooting each other when they don't have to."

⌇

While gangs have grown more fluid in how they associate with rival groups and do business—or don't do business and kill each other—law enforcement on the Lower Mainland has also had its own second thoughts about turf. For its article on the gang war, *The Economist* found its own criminology expert at Simon Fraser, Rob Gordon, who pointed out how gangs work better together than local law enforcement. Gordon reminded the magazine's readers that two agencies designed to crack down on gang activity have been put on the scrap heap since 1998, and he called the current collaborative attempt "riven with conflict."

Sergeant Shinder Kirk of the province's Integrated Gang Task Force admits that there has been a lack of cooperation, but that's in the past. "Certainly when I was first on the streets in Vancouver in the early Eighties, there was this us-versus-them mentality. I'm actually very, very much a proponent of integrated units. I'm very much a proponent of bringing down the silos, if you will, and quite frankly from my personal and professional perspective, those silos— even though there might be the odd hiccup—have crumbled."

As an example of better cooperation, he cites the oddly named, massive investigation in 2007, Project E-Paragon, in which he took part with other officers. The task force, explains Kirk, has "some migration into organized crime, we also have some migration into street-level crime—you just follow the tentacles where they take you."

So investigators for the Combined Forces Special Enforcement Unit in BC, for which he and others were on loan, teamed up with those in the U.S. and other countries. The probe took 14 months to get to the bottom of a drug-smuggling ring in Vancouver and a conspiracy that spanned Ontario, Manitoba, BC, California, Texas, India, China, New Zealand and Australia. Police made more than 100 arrests and seized drugs with a street value of $168 million.

Kirk says as gangs have become more mobile and less territorial, police forces have had to evolve as well.

In the case of Vancouver, it's meant a sharp change in tactics. Inspector Mike Porteous of the Vancouver Police Major Crimes Unit says the force conducted an analysis and found that their "solve rate" for gang-related homicides was lower than the rate at which they were solving regular homicide cases, so they got some experts together and brainstormed. "We decided to employ the same kinds of tactics we would use in a homicide investigation but before the homicide occurred."

The way in which they did that, says Porteous, was an analysis of just who were the most violent gangsters in the Vancouver area, "who were the most likely to go out and shoot somebody tonight." Then they applied investigative resources with the goal of incarcerating those suspects for anything that would get them off the street and behind bars. "Because, obviously, when they're not out there armed in the community, the likelihood of shootings goes drastically down."

Their first incarnation of this "new math" was called Project Rebellion, and it certainly worked when police swooped in on five alleged members of the Sanghera gang who were on their way to attack their rivals, the Bhuttar-Mali group. Instead of slamming the Sangheras over shooting incidents and murders, the suspects faced lesser but still serious charges over possession of weapons, and even charges of breaking and entering for two of the men. Caught in the police net was the alleged gang leader himself, Udham Sanghera.

"Frankly, we are prepared to arrest them on any and as many crimes as we can," Chief Chu told reporters later. "As long as it gets them off the street and into a jail cell, where innocent members of the public can't be hurt, we will continue to pursue them this way."

While Chu and his officers were showing reporters a confiscated cache, which included an assault rifle, bullet-proof vest and several handguns, the RCMP and a list of other municipal forces pulled the same trick on Jonathan Bacon and Dennis Karbovanec, reputed leaders in the Red Scorpion gang. They arrested them in Abbotsford and Port Moody on fraud charges connected to the lease of luxury vehicles.

"Because of the amount of the shootings and gang violence that was occurring out here at the time, I mean, we had to look at it differently," says Inspector Porteous. "Given the toolbox that we have as police officers in this legal system, we have to try things, and if it doesn't work, then we try something else. And this particular strategy clearly did work."

He points out that a core group of gangsters was suspected in about 50 shooting incidents between 2006 and 2008. Thanks to Project Rebellion, he says their rate of shootings has plummeted to zero.

∽

But a downside to the tactic can be expressed in a single word: *bail.* Despite police lobbying against them, three of the five alleged members of the Sanghera gang picked up in the Project Rebellion sweep were soon out, while Bacon and Karbovanec were out the day after their arrests.

Which brings us to the matter of the courts—and this is where the tale of Dennis Karbovanec gets even stranger. When the gang leader stepped into freedom, he put himself in the crosshairs of his enemies, who made an attempt on his life. Ironically, after he received more death threats, police were required to provide around-the-clock protection outside the home of one of the most dangerous gang leaders in the Lower Mainland. The protection detail only stopped when they hauled Karbovanec in on murder charges for his part in the "Surrey Six" homicides.

If police have been justifiably demoralized by such twists or frustrated by the courts, the situation isn't so cut and dried that we can blame the law, either. Sometimes it's perversely complicated. As reporter Kim Bolan pointed out in a feature on gangs for her newspaper, the *Vancouver Sun,* Udham Sanghera was denied bail, while his 31-year-old son, Bobby, was released. Yet when police pulled Bobby Sanghera over, they say he was wearing body armour and carrying three handguns, one of which had the serial number removed.

The reporter herself expressed frustration when she sat on a forum panel organized by the Justice Education Society. Bolan pointed out that while publication bans are supposed to help the accused get a fair trial, they also keep the public in the dark over how the judicial system is coping with the gang problem.

All of this was nothing new for British Columbians. In 2008, two criminologists from Ontario drafted a report commissioned by the BC government. It found that people in the province didn't have much faith in the efforts of their elected representatives or the courts to fight crime. "British Columbians want to understand why sentences in their province tend to be shorter than in other provinces for such crimes as homicide, theft, property crimes, fraud, impaired driving and drug possession."

Only they aren't. The report's authors didn't find substantial difference between how much time you were sentenced to in BC versus a sentencing in, say, Nova Scotia.

They did, however, show that two different judges, handed the same set of facts, could each hand down very different sentences. Still, it's not a fact that encourages public confidence. And one year later, the provincial government announced that it intended to slash $20 million in spending on the police and courts by 2012.

But the picture isn't completely bleak.

Some judges are paying attention to these concerns, at least they are to Mike Porteous. He was optimistic when I spoke to him in the summer of 2009. "It's funny, because you know, if we were chatting about this a year ago or even eight months ago I'd say, yeah, it's frustrating. We put these guys in and they get right back out and then they're up to it again, etcetera, etcetera. But recently, like I would say over the last six months, there's been a change out here. You know, it may be the strength of the cases, or it may be there are some great prosecutors now that are totally onboard, like Teresa Mitchell-Banks. I'm finding now over and over again, these guys are being held in jail."

He's quick to offer a reminder that for the force's Project Rebellion, the courts held all the principals of a targeted gang—none was released on bail.

"The courts out here are now making very, very strong comments and messages in decisions about guns," said Porteous. "And even when we say 'minor offences,' the courts actually take firearms-related offences very, very seriously. You know, if you get caught with a handgun in a car out here, you're looking at federal time."

A word about that federal time. Whatever your political stripe, we all know the Progressive Conservatives like to be known as the "law and order" party (even if they paradoxically don't favour a national gun registry), and Stephen Harper's government has wanted to look tough on rising gang crime. Addressing the Canadian Professional Police Association in 2006, Harper declared, "Parole is a privilege—and it has to be earned." And he followed through on one political promise, to introduce mandatory minimum sentences for serious crimes such as murder.

When a criminal uses a firearm to commit murder, manslaughter, kidnapping, sexual assault or extortion, he gets an automatic minimum four-year sentence. Gun-running earns you an automatic year behind bars. And there are 38 other crimes under the Criminal Code that mean an offender will spend some time locked in a cell. BC Attorney General Wally Oppal backed Harper's move to amend the code, but admitted, "There will be more trials because there'll be less incentive for defence counsel to plead guilty if there's a mandatory minimum sentence. They will feel with some justification there's no percentage in pleading guilty." So be it, was the apparent word from Oppal. He promised his ministry would somehow find the resources to support Ottawa's anti-gang initiative.

Meanwhile, prosecutor Teresa Mitchell-Banks, the head of British Columbia's organized crime prosecution unit, insists that the Crown does its best to lobby for a suspect to be held in custody before conviction when it comes to gun- and gang-related charges. And while some penalties handed down sound ridiculously mild—curfews, no-contact orders and confiscation of a gangster's wheels—these are the kinds of measures that make life more difficult for the organized criminal. As we'll see, police forces and legal authorities in other provinces have taken this same strategy to heart.

Mike Porteous says there was pervasive fear in the Vancouver area, and judges realized this. As a result of what's happening in the courts, for the first time in his recent

memory, people have approached him to offer their grati-
tude. "I would get on several occasions unsolicited thanks
from people for making them feel safe. The public was scared,
and I think the judges knew that. And I think the judges—
who are all very moral people—are saying, you know what,
we need to do our part for community safety as well."

~

When the UK newspaper *The Independent* was
mourning how Vancouver had become a Paradise Lost, it
implied that a simple solution was acknowledged by almost
everyone:

> *In the long run, many British Columbians, on
> both left and right, accept that legalisation and regu-
> lation are the answer. Just the sales tax on C$7bn of
> drugs would pay for several hospitals and schools,
> policing costs could be reduced, property crime by
> addicts to pay for their drug habits would be slashed
> and the gang wars could be quickly reined in.*

There is, however, a flaw in this argument. Criminals
don't like paying sales tax. For gang members, the sale of
illegal drugs is a matter of pure profit. No meddlesome government health authorities checking the quality and safety
of the product, no Revenue Canada demanding you open
your books, certainly no one looking over your shoulder,
seeing how you treat or mistreat "employees."

Inspector Mike Porteous doesn't buy the legalization
argument. "I read a lot of these editorials or some columnists,

and to me it's fairly transparent that they're taking this problem and trying to make it fit into their agenda that they want marijuana legalized. I don't know whether or not the legalization of marijuana will work or won't work, but there are a heck of a lot of other drugs out there that are being sold by gangsters. For example, methamphetamines are *huge*, cocaine is *huge*."

Sergeant Shinder Kirk of BC's Integrated Gang Task Force says that dealers may start with marijuana, since it's easy to grow, easy to obtain and relatively easy to smuggle, but being entrepreneurial, dealers don't stick with that. They turn to whatever will earn a dollar, whether it's cocaine, methamphetamine, Internet fraud or insurance scams. "So really, marijuana is just a small, small component of the overall financial picture for some of these groups."

There is a case to be made that decriminalizing pot would wreck—at least, temporarily—the drug pipeline working its way up from Mexico through the United States. Right off the bat, Canada would knock the economics into a tailspin and rob the trade of a key commodity. So how would gangs up here pay to get all that high-priced cocaine and those weapons?

One possibility is that the harder drugs already in the equation would merely replace cannabis, and there would be a shift of power as those with the most expertise and supply of the new drug flexed their muscles. And so we're right back where we started.

"The key here is the violence, the overt, physical, public violence that we see," says Kirk. "I'm certainly of the view that [decriminalization] will not eliminate that whatsoever." He hates the term "recreational user" of any type of drug and insists there's blood on the product at some point in its journey to the user's hands. Even if you're a casual user, he argues, "You are just as responsible for the violence that we're seeing as if you were pulling the trigger yourself."

Nor would gangs even have to turn to another drug if pot was decriminalized. In his famous book, *Gomorrah*, Roberto Saviano—who must live with a permanent police escort because of what he's uncovered about organized crime—describes the astonishing flow of goods through the port of Naples, Italy, both legal and illegal. "In April 2005," writes Saviano, "the Anti-fraud unit of Italian Customs, which had by chance launched four separate operations nearly simultaneously, confiscated 24,000 pairs of jeans intended for the French market; 51,000 items from Bangladesh labelled 'Made in Italy'; 450,000 figurines, puppets, Barbies, and Spider-men; and another 46,000 plastic toys—for a total value of approximately €36 million. Just a small serving of the economy that was making its way through the port of Naples in a few hours."

There is no debate, of course, over the addictive effects of blue jeans or whether playing with Barbie will lead to wanting "harder" toys.

The gangs go where they can make money and where they can fill a demand, a need.

But what are the needs of the gang member? Besides the motivation of money?

The cliché is that many underprivileged kids drift into a life of trouble and crime because of economic factors and often a brutal home life as well. In other words, they go from victim to gangster. That's true for some. Now meet some gang members for whom this life was a deliberate and conscious choice—and in their minds, *they* are the heroes.

Chapter Two

A Warrior's Religion

ani Amar, a young documentary filmmaker in British Columbia, managed to interview two young gangsters for his movie. They were barely in their 20s when he caught up with them, and in a scenario that gets repeated again and again across the country, the pair began their criminal career selling drugs and illegal weapons in the perfect market-place—high school. As cocky and sure of themselves as they are, Amar says they refused to be interviewed in one location—there was always the chance they might be caught, or at least followed or put under surveillance, or their worst-case scenario, that the filmmaker might betray them and help the police catch them. To get his 90-minute interview, the gangsters drove around four different cities on the Lower Mainland to be safe.

"All these kids think of themselves as high-time gang-sters," says Amar. "They literally look at their lives as gangsters. And I'm talking to them like, 'What do you want to do when you grow up?' They're like, '*This*. This is what we want to do. We want to get to the point where we've become legitimate.'" In other words, so powerful that they become the highest level of organized crime—puppet masters in the Michael Corleone mode. "And this is what they're striving to be."

When Amar came to pick up one of the young men to conduct pre-interview business, he found weapons lying around his subject's bedroom in the family home. Knives, guns, Tasers were all casually strewn on the nightstand and window shelf. "His mom essentially walked in and walked out, saw the weapons and did not give a fuck, did not give a *flying fuck*. Pardon me for my language, but how does a mother walk into a 21-year-old's room, see weapons lying on the night table and walk out without saying a word?"

The young man kept an army-issue, 50-calibre sniper rifle with a laser sight under his bed. "I asked him what is the reasoning for owning a sniper rifle. He immediately told me it is so he can pick off rival drug dealers if they were ever to come to his house. And my argument was, how would you set up a 50-calibre sniper rifle on your balcony in time?"

◇

When the two young gangsters consider their future, they might want to mull over the fate of Bindy Johal. In the 1990s, his name was the one to fear in the Vancouver underworld, and in a way, we have to start with him. And we will come back to Bindy Johal in sometimes surprising ways and in other parts of the country.

His rise and fall makes you think of the criminal friend of the hero in the film, *Slumdog Millionaire,* veering off the screen to walk into Martin Scorsese's *Goodfellas.* Johal, while still in his 20s, ran the largest Indo-Canadian gang in BC, with tentacles squirming into drugs, money laundering, fraud, contract murder and extortion.

His empire's crimes weren't all standard mob fare—some were surprisingly modest in scope but creative. Truckers in Surrey were bribed to rip off their own loads, which would then bring in about $20,000 on the street as stolen merchandise. Johal's thugs purchased wrecked luxury cars in the U.S., hauled them across the border and then removed each car's ignition and its vehicle registration number before the cars were sent to the crusher. The gang members would then go out and steal a matching car, switch the ignition and registration number and auction it off.

His gang earned half a million dollars in its first year. At its peak under his direction, it was taking in about $4 million annually. Part of that empire was the self-proclaimed "Elite," a murder-for-hire squad that charged roughly $20,000 per killing. All the while, Johal had good reason to feel he was untouchable. He walked away with an acquittal after being charged for the murders of two gang rivals, brothers Ron and Jimmy Dosanjh. That his drug business was running headlong into the turf of major competitor, the Lotus Gang, didn't seem to rattle him. He had one high-level Lotus Gang member kidnapped and held for 50 hours until the gang allegedly paid a ransom of five kilograms of cocaine.

In a CBC news footage clip, Johal looks into a camera, addressing his enemies—who they were hardly mattered—and snarls, "Basically, I just want these guys to know you got another thing coming, *bitch*. I'm still around!"

On December 20, 1998, Johal went to the Palladium nightclub in downtown Vancouver without his bodyguards, and while he stood in a crowd of dancing patrons, someone shot him in the back of the head. A bouncer who witnessed the shooting saw that Johal was alive—barely—for a little while afterwards, murmuring words as blood drained from his skull.

There is a disturbing page created in his name on the online social networking site, Facebook, which includes three "fan photos," one of which is a scanned-in newspaper shot of Johal clearly being escorted in the custody of a police officer.

One anonymous insider told a news website in 1999 that the gang leader was a "hero to many young Indo-Canadians" and that his "legend" had spread to Indian communities in other major cities, including American ones. "He stood up to his school principals, he beat up those who called him racial names—and he was making lots of money even though he was in his mid-20s. He drove fancy cars, he had girls falling all over him."

Kash Heed, British Columbia's Solicitor General and a former chief constable for the West Vancouver police, has a less-glowing appraisal of Johal than his hero worshippers. His voice sharpened with clear contempt, he has called Johal "nothing but a gangster who had a very, very short lifestyle....Yeah, he got his face on the six o'clock news. You know what? At the end of the day, he also got his corpse on the six o'clock news. What a way to go."

But as we'll see, Bindy Johal's name is still a source of admiration even beyond Vancouver, the lesson of his grim end completely lost on a few.

～

While Johal was building his empire and becoming a hero to some, Renu Bakshi was growing appalled at the wave of violence. To those living in British Columbia, Bakshi is a familiar face these days as a highly respected television reporter and anchor for CTV News in Vancouver. She graciously agreed to do an interview while on holiday—not to talk about current events, but about recent history, about the horrible days when gang activity claiming Indo-Canadian lives was at its height.

"I did not set out to be a shit-disturber," insists Bakshi. What she saw was making her cry.

"I found myself standing on the side of the road praying. I found the media laughing as we always do at events— that's our defence mechanism." And it is. If you want gallows humour or an irreverent quip to break the oppressive silence of tragedy, walk into a newsroom. "But then I found myself crying and grieving and wondering why."

Bakshi says there was a time when Indo-Canadian men were dying at the rate of one a week. These were her people. This was her community. "And I was on the front lines of covering that. And I got really upset because all I was seeing was our young men slaughtered on the streets. I saw them covered by under-tarps, I saw their blood on the sidewalk, I saw their families come and grieve them and see their bodies lying there."

So in late 2002, the reporter did what reporters do. She wrote an article. In "The Roots of Gang Warfare" published in *Maclean's* magazine, she demanded, "BC's Sikhs must look hard at themselves." It's an elegantly written and deeply insightful piece of journalism. It's also a scathing indictment that sexism, aggression and domestic violence in many Punjabi households in Canada help drive young men into gangs. "From the moment a Punjabi boy opens his eyes, his parents hand him the keys to the Porsche of life," wrote Bakshi. "From now on, his mother will ride in the backseat, literally and figuratively, putting her son ahead of the world. Her boy will have the privilege of eating a warm meal, without the chore of clearing the dishes alongside his sister." She wrote of a bravado culture that included pop tunes encouraging young men to pick up a gun to fight for justice.

Bakshi's article infuriated some, especially those she calls religious zealots. "I clearly stated—*clearly*—that this was a misinterpretation of what Sikhism stands for," that gang kids believed a core idea of the Sikh faith, "Defend the defenceless," meant machine guns and machetes. She admits she took a lot of heat for her article, but she also got the community discussing the issues, perhaps for the first time. And not only about gangs, but also the underlying matter of sexism in Punjabi households. "Ninety-five percent of the community was supporting me, five percent did not—that five percent was extremely vocal."

Since her article in *Maclean's* caused that sensation years ago, Bakshi has been invited to speak at schools, and she says education has changed, but "I don't think family values have changed per se, because you'll always have families who still subscribe to sexism. But, oddly, the gang violence in our community has died down. I mean, I don't see an Indian boy dying at a rate of one a week anymore."

One person who was paying attention to her words was a Punjabi poet and aspiring actor in his 20s living in Burnaby. But instead of sitting in front of a keyboard, Mani Amar picked up a video camera.

∼

Amar was also growing dismayed at the number of youths from his own community winding up in jail or shot dead in the streets of British Columbia's Lower Mainland. What was going on? Why was this happening? Growing up in quiet Port Alberni on Vancouver Island, Amar says he was fairly insulated from both the temptations and the stresses that could have led him to gang life. He looked around to see if any organizations or individuals were tackling the hard questions, "and I came back with my hands empty. There was absolutely nothing being done about this issue."

Amar decided to make a film about it. The result, after three years of investing his own time and his own funds, was *A Warrior's Religion*, a documentary that picked up steam at film festivals across Canada. It won Best Documentary at the Sikh International Film Festival in New York in 2009. At first, the film attracted controversy and resentment at home over its title, which was a reference in part to Bakshi's article and her argument that the values of the Sikh faith were being misconstrued for violent, criminal behaviour. Amar says it was "a war of stupidity" on the part of those who organized protests against his film—people who hadn't even bothered to see it.

While not a practising Sikh himself, Amar certainly grew up in the culture enough to explain its basic tenets, that a Sikh warrior is supposed to be a teacher, a worker, a philosopher and family man first, "and the last thing they will ever be is a soldier...to defend the people that cannot defend themselves. And that is written word for word in our religion. Only then when all else has failed—when all else has failed—will we raise our swords."

But instead of swords raised as a last measure, gang members have drawn guns as their first reaction.

While *A Warrior's Religion* offers more talking heads than compelling visuals, and the filmmaker was clearly still learning as he went along, Amar knew exactly who to zero in on to talk to and how to select his material. Ten minutes into the film, we see Surrey resident Eileen Mohan, who lost her innocent son, Chris, when he got caught in a gang execution in a high-rise building. She holds up a soft cloth bag by the strings. "This is the cover of the urn that carries his ashes," the mother explains for the camera, her voice cracking with grief. "So. This is what a six-foot guy is reduced to…to a case like this." What was once a baby she held in her arms is now only cremated dust she holds up by a drawstring.

Like Renu Bakshi, Amar doesn't let the Indo-Canadian community off the hook for a disproportionate number of its youth causing some of the most horrible mayhem, and the film presents a whole collection of individual opinions. For instance, Jas Sandhu, an addiction counsellor in White Rock—who has a kind of world-weary, jaundiced glint in his eye as he speaks to Amar—points out that immigrant parents make easy fall guys over the gang issue. Yes, these families may face cultural adjustment issues, he says, but they tend to be more liberal than parents who immigrated to Canada in the 1950s, '60s and '70s—an age when Punjabi gangs certainly weren't a problem, if they existed at all.

"So the question is why has this happened the last 10, 15 years? I know there are some people walking around, saying, 'We got to educate the parents. We need parenting workshops.' Well, everyone needs parenting workshops! That's no surprise." To Sandhu, it's "verging on something inappropriate" to suggest that those from another country need to learn parenting skills when they already come from a strong community base.

But contrast that against the point made by Renu Bakshi and others that alcoholism, domestic violence and a prevailing sexism are helping to push young men into gangs. Young Indian men lack for nothing, except the intangibles of self-esteem and proper psychological moulding at home. Most Punjabi gangsters, they say, come from highly affluent families. There is no great want here, no economic deprivation that could possibly be used as a flimsy pretext for thugs-in-training to carve out a stake.

Instead, prominent Sikhs and high-profile Punjabis in the community, in the legislature, in the media and even on the police force have been publicly soul searching, wondering if they haven't unconsciously raised a generation of spoiled brats, young men who want to enjoy the "bling" as something won rather than something earned.

BC Solicitor General and former cop Kash Heed, who gave Amar a stinging epitaph of Bindy Johal for the film, bluntly points a finger at the bravado attitude of young Punjabi men. "Show them the people that are lying in a gutter at two or three in the morning! Show them the people that are lying in a pool of blood at whatever time in a restaurant or in a hair salon or something like that! That's what we should show our community, not these people driving around in their fancy cars....So what, they have money in their pocket—what else do they have? Very little, especially when they're dead on the street."

~

The most pathetic figure in Amar's film is a living postscript to Bindy Johal's saga of mayhem and self-destruction. With sightless eyes behind sunglasses, Bal Buttar sits in a wheelchair, unable to feed or relieve himself and clearly struggling at times for breath. Buttar was once Johal's number-two man, and if he's to be pitied, it's not because of his disabilities, but because he brought them on himself, and worse, because he most likely learned...Not. A damn. Thing.

Buttar grew up in Richmond, a kid who was self-conscious about his attention-deficit disorder and who, naturally, wore a turban, which made him a frequent target of bullies. In elementary school, he was a keen artist, so skilled that teachers compared his work to that of far older students. But Buttar told Mani Amar that at home, he received only ridicule for wasting time with his drawing pencils. His parents scolded him to focus on his math and science homework, that art would get him nowhere. From picking fights at school and stealing from teachers' desks, Buttar soon graduated to stints in youth detention for kidnapping and extortion. Instead of jail making him re-evaluate his life, it merely served as a backdrop for a crucial introduction. It was in a cell that Buttar met the man who would take him further than any of his modest criminal enterprises—Bindy Johal.

Johal took Buttar under his wing, encouraging him to take up bodybuilding and plying him with steroids, and Buttar's standing rose as Johal's success grew. But he eventually noticed changes in Johal, claiming that the gang leader ripped off a few of his associates and started to take stupid chances. According to Buttar, Johal became paranoid around friends.

When he was teased by one of the gang for not wanting to come out and party, Johal casually suggested that members go for a drive and then shot his friend near the Queensborough Bridge. When another frightened gang member wanted to leave, Johal beat him, and it's highly likely he had him murdered. Buttar has claimed that by this time, he realized he had to get rid of the man he had once considered his "brother."

In December 1998, Buttar was riding with Johal on their way to a Surrey nightclub when the gang boss made a U-turn and was pulled over by police. Johal then pulled out a gun, asking Buttar to claim *he* owned it so that he could escape the rap. But Buttar was not a complete fool. There could be only one reason why Johal would risk carrying a weapon—because he was about to eliminate him.

The officer spotted the gun and arrested the pair, but Buttar was already thinking ahead. He now had an alibi as he sat in jail—even as he arranged for the infamous Elite to be paid $20,000 so they would kill his leader. By Buttar's own admission to reporter Kim Bolan, Bindy Johal wound up on a nightclub floor, bleeding out of his skull because of him.

Buttar's own reckoning would come later. In 2001, friends apparently lured him into getting his legs waxed at a beauty parlour on Victoria Drive, where they ambushed him and shot him twice, once in the head and once through the eye. One of his attackers allegedly resented being thrown out of the gang for drug use, while another had begun a romance with Buttar's girlfriend.

"All I remember is a bell, like a wrestling bell," Buttar recalls for the film, his voice floating softly on a weak breath. "*Ding.* Then I wake up…all I see is darkness. All darkness in my eyes."

He was blinded and paralyzed from the chest down.

But even this didn't put an end to his criminal activities, as he allegedly sent the Elite murder squad after gang members who killed his brother. Since then, Buttar has claimed to the *Vancouver Sun* and to others that he found God and wanted to write a book warning young people to avoid falling into gangs. But though he confessed to multiple murders, he had no intention of helping police. "I've never in my life been a rat, and I'll never be one."

And it eventually emerged he might not have changed after all, God or not. In 2007, Surrey RCMP charged Buttar with conspiracy to commit another murder.

The young filmmaker says he was close to being taken in by Buttar's apparent conversion, and in the months that he spoke to the paralyzed gang leader and persuaded him to appear in his film, he tried to help Buttar in his efforts to make a difference, speaking to high school kids, and he even put some of Buttar's notes to paper. "But I always had my gut feeling, and it became stronger as time went on, that he was bullshitting me. His anger would come out of nowhere. He would just snap at me, he would threaten me....You could tell that he was more in love with his shadow, more in love with the person he used to be than the person who he wants to be, and that didn't bode too well. It eventually came out. And you can see the truth now that all he cares about is the notoriety of his name."

Inspector Mike Porteous of the Vancouver Police Department's Major Crimes Unit is blunt in his assessment of the gang leader. "I know him quite well, having deeply investigated him, and I would characterize Bal Buttar as a bona fide psychopath."

As we go to press, Buttar faces a court appearance in the late summer of 2010 over the charge of conspiracy to commit murder.

In the film, Vancouver Police Detective Doug Spencer recalls, "I remember one day talking to Mrs. Buttar, and she said, 'My sons are warriors.' And I went, 'Warriors?' And at the time I'm thinking [as] I drove away, Yeah, your sons are warriors. Well, unfortunately, warriors at war die. And now she's got one dead, one's in the wheelchair, and the other one's floating around, doing all sorts of stuff still. The clock's ticking on him, too."

~

Towards the end of *A Warrior's Religion*, Amar can be seen appealing to a young gangster to rationalize his life, if not leave it altogether. The young man, shown in shadow, is cynical, intelligent and surprisingly articulate. It's clear that their debate will, sadly, go nowhere, and Amar says months later, he ran into his interview subject, who was already moving up in the criminal underworld. Now in the big leagues, he works hand in hand with the Vancouver Hells Angels.

And yet...

Despite one youth lost, the filmmaker can count another in the "Saved" column of the ledger. Amar says he gave "a ton of tickets away" in a school district for a screening of his film in Surrey. One kid's school youth diversity liaison ran into him in Calgary in 2009 when Amar was in town for the Alberta Gang Crime Summit being held at Mount Royal College. The youth was getting involved with gangs and trouble, but when he read in Amar's online bio that he identified himself as a poet and an artist, it started him thinking. The liaison worker told Amar that the young man became interested in philosophy and was turning his life around.

"I was just shocked," says Amar. "I'm like, 'That's awesome.' He saw that he could be confident, and he's chosen to find his passion again. He doesn't want to be a gangster. A lot of these kids have a lack of confidence or insecurity that's perpetuated into violence because they need to have some kind of happiness."

Chapter Three

The Constable

C algary Police Constable Garrett Swihart has seen gang members in the making—and is working hard to pull them back from the brink. He and a colleague, Al Devolin, have been so successful in their efforts that in 2009, Alberta's Solicitor General gave them both an award for their work in the Youth At Risk Development (YARD) program that steps in to help and guide young people at risk of joining gangs.

Previously, Swihart was a School Resources Officer at one of the city's high schools. During his time there, he confiscated enough weapons to fill a hockey equipment bag—knives, guns, brass knuckles, hatchets, baseball bats, tire irons and even a baton with a handle that unscrews revealing a hidden sword. Since YARD, he has switched to youth mentoring for the force.

Like many cops, he is a talented storyteller. He can tell you of meeting one youth who had been in jail 22 times for drug offences, a "neat kid" who clearly hasn't had a break from the moment he left the womb. In fact, the boy's earliest memory as an infant is of watching his father cut cocaine at the kitchen table and sell it out the back door of the house.

You get the impression that Swihart has seen almost every permutation of gang possible: gangs based on ethnicity, on religion, on just about every factor that can help define rival groups. A case in point that disturbs Swihart, especially as he's a father of a First Nations teenager, is how Aboriginal youth are recruiting.

"It's ridiculous to me just because you have a visible difference, maybe more than some others, that means you have to belong. And you say you have to belong to the Indian Posse, now you have to belong to Redd Alert or the Alberta Warriors. It's almost like they're trying to draw sides along lines of anything."

And yet the identities can be fluid. Swihart went to visit one youth in jail who identified himself as a member of a Vietnamese gang—despite the fact that he had blond hair and blue eyes. "You're whiter than I am," Swihart told the kid. "How are you part of this Vietnamese gang?"

The gang member laughed and replied, "Oh, yeah, yeah, yeah! Well, I'm an egg."

Swihart wondered, "What the hell's an egg?"

"I'm white on the outside, yellow on the inside," answered the gang member.

The constable's thought was, *Oh, brother.* Nor was it the last time he's seen gang ethnicity adopted for convenience. "I've seen an African gang where everyone in the group is black except one kid, and the one kid is white, and I'm going, 'Okay.' And the only one that really spent his life in Africa was the white kid!"

The concept of taking on a persona of a completely different nationality just to fit in with a gang strikes him as ridiculous. And yet it is nothing to laugh at when youth have to prove themselves worthy with drive-by shootings and assaults, what Swihart calls the "freak show."

"I see so many getting drawn in, where they say come and join our family, and you know what? My understanding of *family* is totally different from what they're selling."

As a policeman who's also a father, you would expect him to talk about gangs with his own teenage son. Swihart laughs when asked if he has. "He says, 'Dad, I already know this. Dad, you don't have to tell me again!'"

To those on the front lines, youth gang dynamics are ever-evolving, changing weekly and without any lasting structural foundation of leadership. The leader for the week, says Swihart, does the thing that is the most dramatic, that's the most extreme in order to gain respect, notoriety and, if nothing else, a sense of belonging. He says a lot of children are getting drawn away from school, because if they don't find success or acceptance in the community and some job prospects, they make great prospects for a gang.

As in British Columbia, teenagers in Alberta can also step through a looking glass of warped values. Swihart casually approached a group of youths one day on a street corner and asked them the usual, how they were doing, what they were up to. Then he noticed several were wearing T-shirts all carrying a portrait of a familiar face—Al Pacino. And their silver belt buckles bore the name "Scarface." Swihart ribbed them a little about their "old school" tastes until one member pulled him aside.

"Constable," said the gang member in a soft voice, wanting to be taken seriously. "This is Tony Montana." *Not* Al Pacino but Tony Montana, the role Pacino played in the 1983 movie. "He's cool. He's my hero."

Later, Swihart did a little digging and found several pictures of the gang members on the Internet, mimicking stills from the cult film. One sat behind a desk, with a cigar in a large ashtray, the desk holding a white sack of powder as well as a handgun—not a stage prop. It was repulsive to Swihart that this fictional villain (who dies, incidentally, in case you haven't seen the film, drugged out of his skull, shot and floating in a pool) should be their hero. "My hero was Bobby Orr!"

It wasn't long before Swihart was visiting some of these gang members in jail. "You know what? They're following through, being exactly like their hero.... They're being sold a bad bill of goods."

~

While we're on the subject of a bad bill of goods...

A few pages must be spent—not many, but at least a few—on the subject of neo-Nazi gang members. The author does not pretend to be impartial; he is, in fact, the father of a mixed-race child. The question is: how much attention do you give proponents of hate when it may serve their ends more than it creates awareness and fosters investigation of the subject?

The neo-Nazis can't be easily dismissed, especially when considering their progress and insinuation into what are supposed to be legitimate levels of society. Take an international example. In Britain, a member of the right wing, blatantly racist British National Party was elected in 2008 to a London municipal assembly of 25 seats, while two of its members got elected to the European Parliament the next year. Fine, you say, that's Britain; it's far away.

But right at home, we have an operation calling itself a "freedom of expression" group—one that urges you on its website to lobby for Ernst Zundel to be freed in Germany (after Canada finally deported him in 2005) and that advertises a video that claims "Immigration can kill you—literally." For a Fox News report in 2008 on free speech in Canada related to criticisms of Muslims, Fox interviewed this particular leader, identifying him only as a "free-speech activist." He was given American national news coverage, despite regularly spewing hatred against ethnic minorities.

By the way, this man used to be a schoolteacher— before the Ontario College of Teachers finally stripped him of his licence to work in the profession.

But he won't be named here. More on that decision in a moment.

What does this have to do with gangs in Calgary? It has everything to do with it, because a police source suggests that, in his personal opinion, a prominent neo-Nazi leader in the city of Calgary is merely a puppet of this individual in Ontario. One told the other, "Go west, young racist. Proselytize." And so he did around 2006.

We won't name him either.

Their neo-Nazi ideology is being exported across the provinces. One gang, the Aryan Guard, has managed to grab publicity far in excess of its numbers, which the local police estimate only stands at a membership count of about 40, if even that. In 2007, a handful of them stood on the steps of Calgary's city hall, protesting the issue of whether Muslim women wearing burkhas should have to reveal their faces when voting. When the white supremacists marched through downtown Calgary in 2008, a group of 150 anti-racist protesters came out to confront them; screaming matches and scuffles broke out. It made the local papers. It made the national news.

And yet for those in the know, the young men in the Aryan Guard are considered lightweights. Members have been charged over alleged assaults on people belonging to ethnic minorities, but convictions have been difficult to get. "There are threats, there's fear of retribution," says Detective Jas Kainth, who gathered material on the Aryan Guard for the Calgary Police's Criminal Intelligence Unit. "And then there is also that difficulty to prove without a reasonable doubt that the reason the crime was committed was because the victim or complainant was not a white person, or was a Jew."

Kainth has had the opportunity to inspect the Aryan Guard's pamphlets, which members have tried to distribute near schools and in the city's trendy Kensington area, along with their music CDs, which Aryan Guard members have given away outside a large mall. Subtlety is not their strong point, and Kainth says numerology references are common in members' tattoos or writings, such as 14, for the infamous "Fourteen Words"—a propaganda mantra inspired by a long-winded passage in Hitler's *Mein Kampf*: "We must secure the existence of our people and a future for white children."

White kids who may be dealing with issues at home or at school make perfect targets for the Aryan Guard. "If one of the white kids is being bullied by, say, someone of another race, then that'll become the issue—the *race*, not the bullying. And they'll prey on that, and they'll use that. They'll manipulate people, using those thoughts: 'You're a victim, because of race.'"

The manipulation may have variations on the theme, but the goal is the same, and Calgary police certainly define the Aryan Guard as a gang, pointing out that members wear gang colours. Their more obvious branding includes embroidered swastikas or "white pride" logos on flags, and their identity can be found right on their shoes. Those sporting white laces on their black Doc Martins or military boots are supporters. Those with black laces are hangers-on or friends, while those wearing red laces and red suspenders have "drawn blood" for the gang.

They even have their archenemies, the so-called Sharps—Skinheads Against Racial Prejudice. But police say anti-racist skinheads aren't doing the community any favours, acting as a gang themselves by engaging the Aryans in a long-running, sometimes violent feud. The two groups hate each other and have had several nasty clashes. Kainth says that Sharp activity, however, has recently been on the wane.

He also concedes that while members are few, the Aryan Guard is acting as a way station for disturbed, anti-social and thuggish youths, those who may not stick around but could always graduate to more serious criminal activity. He knows one young man who interrupted his drug-dealing career for three and a half months while he was a member of the Aryan Guard—they apparently frown on drugs, or at least publicly disapprove of them (but don't disapprove so much of beating the crap out of a homeless Aboriginal person). Eventually, Kainth says, the youth gave up on the Guard—and went back to dealing drugs.

So the search goes on for new recruits. Which brings us back to Constable Garrett Swihart. He tells the story of one 16-year-old boy recruited at a concert, who was supplied with alcohol and "free women." He practically disappeared from home, and Swihart says it took two months before he could track the young man down. To reach the boy, he had to ask around for the Aryan Guard's leader, and a meeting was arranged—the gang members wouldn't let the constable meet the boy alone.

Swihart sat across a coffee-shop table, passing on messages from the youth's mother and relatives, talking about how the kid could get help with school, activities, a job, and how obviously the boy's family still cared about him. "Every time I'd mention one of the family members and tell him the message that I was to relay, his face would light up, beautiful smile and his blue eyes would just shine... and all of a sudden he'd put his head down real quickly when he would look into [a gang member's] eyes. That's how controlling it was."

Six months later, the boy was out of the gang, but lasting damage had been done. "He can't go back to his mom's house because one of the Sharps lives a block away." And as large as Calgary's LRT system is, the boy doesn't dare use it in case he runs into a member of one faction or another.

Swihart became a thorn in the gang's side, quietly demanding to know about the boy's safety while he was within their ranks. He learned that the youth had wound up serving as practically a housemaid for the leadership, their psychological control resembling that of a cult. Nor was the gang willing to easily give up their new recruit, as Swihart discovered when one high-ranking member made a carefully veiled threat over the phone to him.

"I made notes of it," says Swihart. "He said, 'Gee, a lot of people seem to know a lot about me. Thought I should start learning a lot about *you*.'" The gang member then rattled off details about the constable's father and family.

In the end, charges weren't laid, and Swihart says it turned out to be a good experience because he went to his force's security operations and learned just how much of his life was there on the Internet for all to see. The gang member "hadn't made mention of my wife's name, fortunately for both of us…"

Making a threat, veiled or overt, to a police officer is probably not the smartest move, but Swihart's colleague, Jas Kainth, doesn't consider this particular gang member terribly articulate or bright. "He's not exactly the sharpest knife in the drawer. Not by any stretch." Officers on the Calgary police force take great delight in the fact that white supremacists have had to deal with Detective Kainth, a practising Sikh who wears a turban in accordance with his religion. Kainth describes the reaction of the high-ranking Aryan Guard member when they first met: "It totally threw him for a loop."

But we won't mention the name of that member.

Or any of the leadership.

Or the name of their fellow hate-monger in Ontario.

Or anyone else in these racist organizations.

Their opinions, of course, are available on their websites and on YouTube videos. The names of specific high-profile members will have to wait until actual charges are laid, and charges were never laid against the member who made that veiled threat against Constable Swihart. To name any of them in a nationally distributed book is to give them more power, which seems to be their ultimate goal.

It can be argued that the neo-Nazis can then still spread their intellectual poison quietly, handing out their CDs and pamphlets to impressionable youngsters. We have schools to remedy such ignorance. The Calgary force's Criminal Intelligence Unit can keep an eye on them, and there is no need to create a journalistic "balance" by airing their views that can't stand up to the simplest historical scrutiny. Since their main threat is in ideas, they are arguably the weakest of gangs because they lack ammunition.

And so their leaders won't be named here. We have guardians to protect us against their violence, and we always need more good teachers to protect us against brain rot. And with a bit of luck, the hate-mongers will slowly but inevitably fade away.

∾

Kids who have mentors and role models—perhaps a sports coach, a music teacher or a caring family uncle—stand a better chance. On a cold page, this sounds like a pathetically bland idea in its simple common sense. But when you confront the facts of life for children at risk, the simple truth takes on a desperate urgency. "Those kids are more resilient to the pressures of being involved in a gang than any of the gang members I've seen," says Garrett Swihart.

To do his job, the constable doesn't wear a uniform or drive a marked police vehicle when he visits the home of a troubled youth. He stresses over and over again that the work is about building relationships and rapport.

"My goal hasn't been to harass. My goal and purpose in my work is to try to keep youth out of the criminal justice system," says Swihart. "So all of a sudden, the youth is going, 'Whoa, this is a little different policeman, and he's talking to me in a manner that is different than how they've been talked to before.' And you treat them as young men and young women and say here are some of the choices, this is where it's leading you and try to educate them or empower them to understand the choices that they're making..."

When meeting with youth and their families, Swihart tries to outline some of their options. It could mean he speaks to a principal over a suspension, or maybe a teenager goes to school in the morning but leaves at noon to be able to keep a job. He says it comes down to what the youth need and where they have a deficit, as well exploring what the community can provide.

"A lot of the youth we see, if something goes haywire at school, kicking them out for three to five days doesn't help them, it just solidifies their involvement and negative contact with the gangs, if that's what they're doing. It just helps them to be drawn even deeper into the gang."

In one case, Swihart recalls, a mother had fled Sudan and lived for eight years in a refugee camp in Kenya, where her two children were born, before coming to Canada. Then the threat was no longer from the myriad factions and the brutal regime in Khartoum, but from an older Sudanese male who accosted one of her sons on Calgary's LRT. "Will you sell drugs for me today?" he asked the 12-year-old boy.

The dealer literally put it that way. An invitation and a threat combined in one question. Refuse, and the boy faced a beating—each and every time he dared to cross a particular station on the LRT.

While the mother could have moved with her son into a new neighbourhood, that wouldn't end the risk for her son. And coming from a country where an Arabic regime brutalizes and tries to exterminate its own black citizens to plunder the southern half of the country for resources, the mother was naturally suspicious of police. Swihart says that if she heard the police coming, she slammed the door.

So he enlisted the help of the bishop at the mother's church.

"I would never have gotten in that door without that good bishop and the relationship there."

When Swihart spoke for this book, the boy had been involved with the YARD program for about a year and was about to take a week-long trip to a mountain-bike camp. He was involved in skiing, basketball, Scouts and had a "wonderful" mentor. "This young man now has a whole lot of people in his corner that he doesn't want to disappoint," says Swihart. "His mom made a comment to me just a couple of weeks ago, she goes, 'He's a good boy now.'"

Of course, the stories of the roughly 50 youths that have come and gone through the program don't all have movie-of-the-week happy endings. Some teens have graduated and moved on, some are still involved, some "have failed to follow through on what's been asked of them." Swihart quickly adds, "And I'm not giving up on any of those ones that have been unsuccessful so far."

Like Eileen Mohan mourning her son, the police are faced with a reality that at times seems surreal and macabre, outstripping *Scarface* or any of the mob movies the impressionable teens are so keen to emulate. Take a young man Constable Swihart knows who considered Bindy Johal a hero and who boasted he would be bigger than his criminal idol. How to get through to him? When the Calgary Police's anti-gang website, www.getalife.ca, featured a video interview with a relative of a gang member, he thought he might have found an Exhibit A.

Swihart called up the ambitious young Johal-wannabe and insisted they meet one night, even calling in an "IOU" to get the kid to see him. At a Tim Horton's coffee outlet, Swihart played the video on a laptop computer. There on the screen was Nina Rahal.

"She's beautiful," said the young man. "Who is she?"

Nina Rahal is indeed beautiful, but what mattered was that she was the sister of gangster Jaspreet Singh Rahal, who was shot dead in 2005, only a few seconds after he walked out of a gym on his way to his Lincoln Navigator SUV. There were at least six shell casings where he fell. His murderers clearly intended to make a thorough job of it. Nina Rahal was on the video, relating how hard it was for her brother to leave the life and what a nightmare it became for her family.

"You know, you never think your brother's going to get shot," she says on camera. "You never think that. You're just thinking, okay, he's home now, he's distant, I mean they're going to forget about him...." She describes how her brother's so-called friends didn't bother to visit the grieving family after his death, but hours after Jaspreet Singh Rahal was left lying cold on a Calgary street, they picked through his belongings at his condo before relatives could collect precious keepsakes and reminders.

As it became clear exactly what the video was for, Swihart sat across from the young man at their table and told him, "I don't want to go to your funeral. You understand that?"

But the message was slow to sink in. Two weeks later, in the early morning hours of a Saturday, the youth was shot in a car, while one of his friends was killed and another badly wounded. The young man who thought he was going to be bigger than Bindy Johal was hunkered down in the passenger seat, bullets drilling through the car's door to rocket up his tailbone into his body. Swihart got a call at 5:30 in the morning and was soon in the hospital, hugging the gangster's distraught mother.

But Swihart will accept victories when he can get them. Like when a gang member called him up, saying, "Constable, I need your help." He told Swihart that he saw younger kids making bad choices, the kind the officer had tried to warn him about. At an East Indian restaurant, Swihart was able to negotiate the hand over of two sawed-off shotguns. No raid. No arrests. But the guns are off the street.

It speaks to the admiration the constable has slowly garnered among gang members.

Swihart has developed respect as well for those he's trying to reach. "These guys, they have honour. It may be displaced a little bit. I've heard a lot of people say these gang kids are thugs and rats—they use names like 'vermin' to call them. Well, most of these young guys are my friends. You build relationships. Yeah, you care for them, they're people.

Some of these situations that they get involved in are situations they don't have power over."

Years ago, Swihart was up in the stands for a basketball game at a high school, having brought along his wife and his then 10-year-old son. He was suddenly called to deal with a situation that had erupted at the school. "And so I had to split to go deal with a problem…and I've got these fairly hefty heavy-hitters up in the stands, and I'm turning to them and go, 'You guys take care after my family?'"

"Absolutely, Constable," one of them replied. "*Nobody* will bother them."

As it turned out, one of the youths he asked would be the gang member who turned over the shotguns.

"They would defend my family with their lives," insists Swihart. "I really believe that."

And so the relationships grow and evolve, as relationships do, even with troubled young people in gangs. Swihart says he's made his share of trips to hospitals and attendances at funerals. "I've been to the graduations, too. I've had one young man call me up and say, 'Constable, what are you doing in April?'" Swihart says he laughed and replied, "I don't know, Justin, what am I doing in April?'

"And he says, 'Will you come to my wedding?'"

Chapter Four

The New Wild West: Calgary

They started in high school. *High school*, where you're supposed to worry about trigonometry tests and whether you'll go to the basketball game Friday and if you really love Melissa Deol because the two of you have done it once and it felt kind of good but awkward, but at least you weren't stupid like James who *didn't* wear a condom his first time (loser). Only she just shrugged and said thank you when you handed her the mix CD you made for her.

You remember high school, right? The place where you can get cocaine, Ecstasy, hash, methamphetamines, and, oh yes, illegal weapons.

Many parents are well aware today that their kids attend a different kind of school than what they went to.

Drugs can ruin their lives. Sex too early can often ruin their lives. But even the gangs of a bygone age were supposed to be more concerned with mindless vandalism and boosting cars than serious crime.

For a while, it seemed true enough of the Vietnamese teenagers hanging out together at Forest Lawn High School back in the late '90s, a pre-9/11 era in which the biggest and most ridiculous calamity expected to hit the world was Y2K. The immigrant parents of these teens, some who had survived the horrors of war and slaughter in Vietnam and Cambodia, were often out of the house, working to try to make ends meet. Meanwhile, their kids were using cigarettes and coins to burn tattoos into their hands and arms. One familiar design stands for the five Vietnamese *Ts* of the criminal underworld: *tinh* (love), *tien* (money), *tu* (prison), *toi* (crime) and *thu* (revenge).

The Forest Lawn High School gang made connections with teens at other high schools and built a thriving trade in "dial-a-doping"—just call a cellphone number to arrange a drug transaction. As easy as ordering a pizza. They called themselves "Fresh Off the Boat," or FOB. Since the days of the big influx of refugeees from Vietnam and Cambodia, it's been a derogatory term, one often used by Asians who are more established or who at least were born in Canada. Like other marginalized groups, the gang members were taking the name back and making it their own.

Then something happened. No one seems to be completely sure what, except for a handful of veteran gang members within the inner circles—a dispute over a girlfriend, or someone stealing drugs or a personal item like a watch that didn't belong to them. But the days of easy money and camaraderie were over. Now there are two groups, the FOB and the "Fresh Off the Boat Killers," or FK. It's an old axiom that the bloodiest feuds are the ones between families.

In February 2002, war literally broke out on the streets of downtown Calgary, right outside a karaoke bar, and it claimed innocent lives.

Vuthy Kong of the FK stabbed Adam Miu, who wasn't in either gang. As that was going on, the FK's John Pheng was swinging a baseball bat into the skull of Miu's brother. Kong was later convicted of manslaughter for Miu's death, while Pheng pleaded guilty to a charge of assault. Though Miu was a "civilian," the attack on him only made tempers boil hotter. And the two factions had their own ideas about administering justice for the fight in the street.

Two days before Christmas 2002, an FK gang member, Linju Ly, drove past the Chapters bookstore at Southcentre Mall while his passenger, Michael Oduneye, stuck a handgun out the window and fired four shots, severely wounding Jason Youn. Six days later, the FOB hit back, shooting one FK associate dead inside a busy nightclub and then killing Linju Ly right in front of his parents' house in

Renfrew as he shovelled snow. And the tit-for-tat bloodshed went on. One FOB associate, Mathew Anderson, just 19, was killed during a Chinatown street fight in 2004, while John Pheng met his end inside another nightclub on 17th Avenue SW the following year.

Then something happened on New Year's Day 2009 that sparked a wave of public outrage over gang violence in Calgary.

~

Unless you live in Alberta, you have probably never heard of Keni Su'a. Just for the record, he was a 43-year-old construction worker who came to Canada from Samoa. According to his ex-wife, he was a quiet, reserved fellow— a man who liked rowing and rugby, had a brilliant sense of humour and was one of those people who was a great friend with decent values, who probably would never make the news unless he won Lotto 649 or something bad happened to him. Something bad did happen, just as the brand-new year got started, and all because he went for lunch at Bolsa, a Vietnamese restaurant at Calgary's Macleod Trail and 94th Street SE.

Sources told the *Calgary Herald* that Aaron Bendle, who bought small amounts of cocaine for himself and to resell, was abducted at gunpoint by men who wanted to kill his drug contact, FK member Sanjeev Mann. Bendle, who wasn't a gang member, set up a meeting with Mann at Bolsa in the afternoon because his kidnappers had threatened his family. When the gangsters marched into the restaurant to gun down Bendle and Mann, Keni Su'a saw what was happening and escaped out the door.

The assassins chased him and shot him in the back, beating and kicking their target before he died in a parking lot.

"The thought of being shot in the back, first of all, you know, is pretty terrible," his ex-wife, Lenni Folden-Su'a, told CBC Calgary. "But he was unarmed, like he had no weapon on him whatsoever, and they chased him down just in cold blood and murdered him that way, and it's been really hard to accept that."

As this book goes to press, police charged three men over the murders and were tracking down a fourth.

The associations and carnage in Calgary's gang war have grown so complicated that the *Herald* designed a flow-chart, indicating those alive in white boxes and those dead in black boxes. The death count was up to 25 when the chart was published in March 2009, and it didn't even include those who had been wounded. And keep in mind, that's just for *two factions*. At any one time, Calgary police are keeping their eyes on roughly 400 gang members and their associates, who belong to various groups.

Calgary Herald reporter Jason van Rassel says the structure of FOB and FK now transcends the people, with FOB in particular decimated either by members put in jail or killed. Those who are in the gang now are continuing the grudge. While they might have family members connected or a small personal stake, they certainly weren't around for the original dispute a decade ago. "I've likened it to—obviously on a way smaller scale and a way shorter period of time—almost Northern Ireland." As in the Catholics and Protestants who were constantly fighting; blind zealots fixed in their beliefs.

Van Rassel has written scores of gang and crime stories for the *Calgary Herald*. Affable and keenly observant of what's happening in his city, he knows his subject matter. So much so that the Calgary police force will actually refer a journalist to *him* to get the pieces of a puzzle on which they don't want to comment.

According to van Rassel, in 2002, a task force called Operation Synergy put a lid on the violence between the two groups for the better part of two and a half years as members all went down on drugs and weapons charges— but that only kept them off the streets of Calgary for two or three years. Now that many are back and new recruits are coming in, he has watched the gangs reinvent themselves.

"They seem to be very aware of—for lack of a better way of putting it—branding...I can tell you that people within FOB now rarely refer to the gang as Fresh Off the Boat. The acronym has actually come to mean different things over the years. They've evolved the brand to reflect the multicultural aspect of the gang."

While the FOB name has been kept, van Rassel says the initials can now stand for "Forever Our Brother" or "Fresh Out of Bullets." And that's even prompted a corresponding response from the *Herald*. "We've officially stricken 'Fresh Off the Boat' right out of our [house] style whenever we write about the gangs."

So with perhaps no conscious intent, let alone notice, FOB has become a criminal institution that needs to be included in a newsroom's style guide. The group has made some of the biggest headlines, but for all their violence, gang activity on the whole was on a decline as this book went to press.

"I think there was a feeling in this city, particularly around 2008, that you know, things were getting out of control," says van Rassel. "The police have devoted an unbelievable amount of resources into suppressing the violence and for the most part right now—I mean we have no way of knowing what's going on behind the scenes—things seemed to have calmed down."

He says that local people are happy in the main with the police. "The large degree of frustration you see from the public here in Alberta is with the justice system. You know the phenomenon is called 'catch and release.' They get arrested, released on bail conditions, and then they're picked up with an arsenal of weapons cruising around with their buddies three weeks later. And that has bred a lot of, I'd say, frustration and mistrust with the legal system."

Meanwhile, it seems, the gangs keep evolving. While his paper published a flowchart for readers, van Rassel keeps a spreadsheet just for his own reference with about a hundred names on it. "These groups are so amorphous and so fluid that I don't really, rightly, get hung up on who's a member and who's an associate....You're not dealing with a huge pool of people, but it's a significant one."

Top cops will tell you that the gangs in Calgary, for the most part, don't sport colours or specific clothing, nor do they have set territories. If the West Side of downtown Saskatoon or the North End of Winnipeg is infamous for certain factions, it's not the same in the home of the Stampede. And the gangs have grown in sophistication when it comes to methods of murder. One shooting victim never saw his killers at all—because like Russian soldiers in World War II, they had camouflaged themselves in white clothing to hide in the snow banks. Gang members will go out and buy GPS trackers to place on the vehicles of victims, hunting their prey with a laptop as they drive along, waiting for the right lethal moment. They will use convoys to distract with staged accidents. They will walk into department stores to buy "kill kits," which include cheap, disposable clothing to avoid leaving forensic evidence.

Gangs are nothing if not adaptable. Associations with groups outside the province don't have to be formal; they can be a matter of convenience when it comes to getting hold of some of the lucrative cocaine coming up from Mexico and through the Lower Mainland of British Columbia. Sometimes, however, the lines blur altogether. Local authorities consider at least half a dozen members of the FK to be members of British Columbia's UN gang. In fact, a couple of FK members served as bodyguards for a UN leader.

The gangs sometimes defy expectations, though the model of the legitimate business economy is always a clue for forecasting. Methamphetamines, for instance, did not become the full-blown crisis in the city that observers thought it would, and Jason van Rassel says the reason is good business sense, something his police contacts pointed out to him. Meth is, after all, a very cheap drug to purchase, one that keeps you high for a long time.

"So if you're a guy dealing crack here in Calgary, making money hand over fist, why would you switch to a drug that will basically cost people less and keep them high longer?"

He's naturally had opportunities to speak to a few gang members himself. "It would be easy to underestimate them as inarticulate, you know, because they're not the most articulate guys in the world, the ones I've met. Some of them have a bit of a slavish devotion to U.S. hip-hop kind of lingo. So it could be easy to…laugh at them as imitators because they want to talk like 'gangstas'….The thing is, though, when you take a deeper look and you go beyond those first impressions, both gangs have a level of sophistication that really belies these guys on an individual basis, how inarticulate and volatile and seemingly dumb they can be."

The sophistication of the gangs was demonstrated last year when police raided a Heritage Pointe house in a drug bust. They were shocked to discover that a suspect had an internal police document from 2005, a list of FK members complete with mug shots and names of officers to use for identification.

Calgary police officials have been candid over the leak, pointing out that the document didn't have any addresses or other information that could have compromised individuals or cases. The force's Integrated Gang Enforcement Team conducted an internal investigation, but it never found out how the document got into the open. Acting Staff Sergeant Gordon Eiriksson of the Organized Crime Operations Centre admits frankly, "It could have been stolen from a police facility. You know, our vehicles get broken into just like everyone else's—we don't know."

And what about the possibility that someone on the force handed it over? Eiriksson says, "That could always be speculated, but I certainly don't think that was the case. If that was the case, then there would certainly be a plethora of additional information that could be provided. However, that's all that we found."

But it's a disquieting thought that the gang was able to obtain it at all. Like law enforcement, gangs can build their own intelligence networks.

≈

Calgary Police Chief Rick Hanson has gone further, comparing gang members to terrorists. At an Alberta Gang Crime Summit in 2009, he argued that there *are* similarities, and that Canadian police forces and legal authorities should take a more international view, watching for trends abroad and in the U.S. Hanson told the *Herald* that both gangs and radicals offer impressionable young men a mirage of certainty in beliefs. "Greed is usually the last reason somebody gets involved in a gang."

The similarities don't end with recruitment. When shootings and gang violence were at their most frequent, Calgary citizens didn't feel safe going out to bars or nightclubs. That does, indeed, sound like urban terrorism to Acting Staff Sergeant Eiriksson. "I'll venture to argue that the gang members that we talk about certainly would not want to be cast in the same pool as the terrorists. But I think it's an issue more of the mentality and the absolute lack of ethical behaviour and the lack of moral fibre and just ommon decency...."

This lack of ethics extends to other gang members. "There's this false sense of camaraderie and brotherhood, and it's interesting, because we *know* from our investigations that these groups don't trust each other," says Eiriksson. "The people from within the same group don't trust each other. If somebody gets arrested, they're immediately suspect—[they think] that person was going to become an informant. Or somebody else gets arrested, they're wondering who from within their own group might have talked to the police to result in that arrest. So what happens to this high level of brotherhood and solidarity? It goes out the window."

Just like terrorists, say police, the more veteran gang members prefer to be invisible, even respectable. They can be well mannered, well dressed, drive nice vehicles and live in affluent neighbourhoods. Eiriksson says if he showed you 30 pictures of individuals and asked you to pick out the gang members from the regular civilians, you couldn't do it. Those living on quiet residential streets are likely shocked when a neighbour's name or photo ends up in the media or they see them dead on the pavement. "Gang members are everywhere."

And the gangs study their enemy. Eiriksson points out, "Whenever we conduct an investigation with disclosure, we're educating the criminals as to how we do business." Gang members become aware of police methods of surveillance, undercover work and investigation. They don't want to make the same mistakes again.

Law enforcement, he insists, has to try to match the gangs in their growing sophistication within a legal framework. Gang members travel freely, and well, yes, so can the police, but they can only *afford* to do it a few times a year. Investigations take months, even years, with officers racking up overtime and the tab coming due for resources.

To make his point when he gives talks or presentations, Eiriksson likes to use a video of a drive-by shooting that took place in the United States. Four gang members in a car drive up to a victim walking along a sidewalk. They shoot him, and then one gets out of the car and fires five shots into their target to finish the job. As the gang member hops back into the vehicle, the car speeds away for their escape. The gang members shot the brief video themselves as a trophy—conveniently supplying the cops with evidence. American authorities got hold of the footage thanks to a search warrant. ("Idiots" is the term Eiriksson uses for the gangsters.)

"So I use this video in my actual PowerPoint presentation because I show people—look, this video lasted 11 seconds. You know how much that 11 seconds is going to cost us? The guys are going to be away from their families for weeks at a time. That is going to take eight months to a year for us to solve based on *11 seconds* of violence. The gang members don't care because the guy's dead. Mission accomplished. That's when our real job begins: trying to put those pieces together."

It's been as steep a learning curve for Calgary police as it's been for other forces across the country, and Eiriksson admits the force was slow to respond to the threat. "I don't think we got in front of it soon enough." But now, "We've taken our heads out of the sand," and forces are talking to each other, developing integrated units and investigative strategies. "And we're seeing that here in Calgary because the violence has dropped. It's like the stock markets in November [2008], it just plummeted."

That has spelled more cooperation and confidence from the community. "Previously, the attitude may strictly have been well, what's the point of talking to the police because they never arrest anybody anyways? Well, now we're able to show, yeah, with your help, we can arrest them, we can put them in jail, we can make them accountable. So this will only help to propel us forward, of getting more buy-in and involvement and cooperation from the public."

Chapter Five

The New Wild West: Winnipeg

The North End of Winnipeg has always been seedy and dilapidated, but in the past there were always families happy to live there, getting by, often Aboriginal or from a mixed bag of immigrant ethnicities. There seemed to be an invisible border at the Museum of Man and Nature, and the neighbourhood ran on the fumes of its glory days from the early part of the 20th century, way back to when leftist Jews lived there and fought the good fight to win more union concessions and rights for the working man.

Today, the North End is, by anyone's measure, worse—an inner-city war zone to rival those of America, and the West End is catching up fast. In the summer of 2009, two gangs—MOB and the Indian Posse—were waging a battle for turf with innocent residents caught in the middle. A 13-year-old boy saw gunplay happen right in front of him as he walked along with his nine-year-old sister. He told the CBC that he was careful about the colours he wears, often settling on a neutral black, so that he doesn't get misidentified as a member of a rival faction. "If I wear red around here, I'll get shot or something."

The realities of violent life in the North End are so obvious that even a five-year-old can see them, as one little girl has, telling the reporter she sees "lots of cops" in her neighbourhood. Another girl, just 11, wished her neighbourhood was different and that in her daydreams, "it would be nicer."

And as you consider that, think of the name Hussein Jilaow. If you don't live in Winnipeg, it won't mean anything to you. It barely means anything to most people there now. But there's a reason why the name is being mentioned in connection with children who can't even play outside and who learn almost from the time they sit on tricycles that they could easily, carelessly, thoughtlessly, get hurt by kids who are strangers, ones barely older than themselves.

~

Winnipeg has a reputation for Native youth in gangs, with groups such as the MOB and Indian Posse. But Staff Sergeant Rhyse Hanson of the Winnipeg police's Criminal Investigation Bureau doesn't like the term "Aboriginal gangs." He considers it a disservice to the Aboriginal community, and like Garrett Swihart, he is quick to point out that some gangs may be made up of mostly Native members, but they can include non-Aboriginals as well.

In truth, Winnipeg has become the "Gateway to the West" for a variety of different gangs, not just ones that have a majority of Native youth. Here, too, as in Calgary with the FOB, members can lose track of their own organizational history. The MOB now have a laundry list of explanations for their name. Colours can be worn here—one gang, for instance, favours red baseball caps with the letter *B* like the kind worn by fans of the Boston Red Sox. Here, violence flares up over turf, drugs, a dispute involving someone's girlfriend or even the wrong look.

As with Keni Su'a in Calgary, Winnipeg, too, was outraged over the murder of an innocent. In October 2005, Phil Haiart, only 17 and a popular graduate of St. John's Ravenscourt School, was walking with a friend near the corner of Sargent Avenue and Maryland Street in the West End. It was around 11 o'clock at night, and the two young men stumbled into a shooting gallery. Two rival gangs were having it out near a crack house on McGee Street. Haiart was shot in the stomach, while his friend got hit in the forearm, and they tried to run away from the scene. Haiart collapsed to the filthy street, bleeding his life away, and a passing driver managed to get the attention of a police cruiser. The boy died in hospital four hours later.

Things have not gotten better. On a Friday night in July 2009, one gang went on a spree in the North End;

it began at around 6:30 at night, and as Rhyse Hanson puts it, the gang's members "just basically attacked everything that moved before they were finally arrested." One of the gang's eight victims was a 60-year-old man. Another was a single father of three who was quite literally making a milk run along Aikins Street—the gang intercepted him, punching him in the head. A knife persuaded him to hand over the $60 he planned to use to buy diapers for his youngest son.

"It's not the 20-year-olds you have to be worried about anymore," the father told the *Free Press*. "It's the 15- and 16-year-olds. It's like they're devolving. They're the kind who will stab you after they've already stolen your money."

Only minutes before the father's brush with the gang, 24-year-old Joseph Hall had run into them minutes away from the safety of his own residence. He was stabbed and left to die in the street, but somehow got back to his home, where he died in his mother's arms. Two days later, the news hit the papers that the police had charged four gang members with manslaughter and robbery.

~

In the lunar landscape of the −35°C winters and the crumbling West End, those born in completely different climates, with completely different languages than our official ones, are doing their best to cope. Find jobs. Raise families. Get by. Somalis. Sudanese. Ethiopians. Eritreans. And more. Some of their children, scarred by the war zones of home, are recreating hell on earth along pathetic, broken stretches of West Broadway.

The Mad Cowz came to the forefront around 2004, cornering the West End market for crack distribution. The gang actively looked for refugee children, ones who had seen bloodshed first-hand and who knew how to use guns. A year later, the African Mafia—with members mainly from Sudan and Somalia—were on the scene. Youth who witnessed massacres, who had to fight to survive and reach refugee camps thousands of miles away, have made ripe pickings for the gangsters in Winnipeg. The disaffected youngsters often have trouble in school, both with the language and being put into the wrong grade where they can't cope with—let alone, understand—what's expected of them for homework assignments.

A former gang member of the Mad Cowz told *Maclean's* magazine in 2007 that the African Mafia grew out of young boys wanting to socialize with those they could relate to. "They're told, 'You're going to move to Winnipeg. You're going to go to school and have a future,'" he says. "But they move to the west side, to Central Park. They barely speak English. There's nothing they can relate to. They walk around like little zombies. It's only a matter of time before they get drawn in."

He offered a chilling insight into the gang's recruiting tactics. "We watch them. Once it looks like they're ready, we go to them. We have big, fancy cars and gold chains—we sell them dreams."

~

By now, you have most likely forgotten the name referenced earlier—Hussein Jilaow. His life was brief, violent and pointless, unless a point is assigned to it. He was a member of the Mad Cowz, buying dreams that didn't ring with a jangle of gold but with the metal hum of cell bars. Jilaow became a sociopathic gangster like Bindy Johal, but because he was never as successful, no one has devoted a Facebook or MySpace page to him lately.

By the time he was 25 years old, Jilaow had been convicted of 13 offences—assaults, robberies, threats. He liked switchblades. He liked to use them. And when a knife wasn't handy, no problem. Two Winnipeg cops who once broke up a fight in which Jilaow was involved watched him bite his own lip hard enough to bleed and then spit at them. "I'm HIV. I'll give you HIV."

Jilaow was tossed into a jail cell for assault and soon fell out with the other inmates. Whatever the grudge was, the guards had to use pepper spray on him, and a furious Jilaow barked to one of them, "I'll kill you and rape your wife!" He declared to another, "I'm not afraid of coming back to jail for killing a guard—it will be worth it." He earned himself a three-year prison sentence for intimidating justice officials.

Why should anyone care about Hussein Jilaow?

Once upon a time, there were those who did. Jilaow was born in 1980 into the hell that Somalia had become through civil war. When he was 11 years old, he saw his father shot dead by a sniper in Mogadishu, and after becoming a refugee along with several members of his Marehan clan, he first managed to get into the United States and then into Canada. The boy couldn't say where his mother and his five siblings were. Winnipeg Child and Family Services found him downtown and mistook him for an Ethiopian, so they contacted the owner of an Ethiopian restaurant who had founded a community organization. Fortunately, the man's wife was fluent in Somali. The boy had a home for a while, living with the couple and their three children.

But he did not find peace. Young Hussein suffered from post-traumatic stress disorder caused by his war experiences, screaming himself awake from violent nightmares that prompted him to "get up from bed and sit by himself." One teacher called him a nice boy but one who was "obviously troubled." He spoke little English and his education was hopelessly behind those of his age group at John Pritchard School.

At 17, he had dropped out of school and left the house of his adoptive parents, working as a drug runner for the Mad Cowz. He was also a consumer of the product, both using and dealing crack. He couldn't keep a job. His girlfriend gave birth to his son, Mohamed, but when she left him, she cut off his contact to their son. He was homeless at 19, and with its cruel winter, Winnipeg is one of the last cities where anyone would ever want to sleep rough. If it was too cold for Jilaow to sleep near an Ellice Avenue 7-Eleven, he would wander the downtown core and warm up with a coffee at Mac's. Jail turned out to be the most reliable shelter he would have.

To the authorities, he was vicious and probably irredeemable. The question was whether or not to deport him. In Winnipeg, the young man had found an identity with the Mad Cowz gang, a group he chose. If he went back to Mogadishu, everyone was aware he would be in danger because of tribal politics and his clan, which was in hiding at the time—a clan that, unlike his gang, he never had a choice to belong to.

"His violence has escalated, and there is every reason to believe it will continue to do so," conceded Federal Judge Sean Harrington when he ruled on the case. "Mr. Jilaow does not come to the Court with clean hands. However, that is no reason to send them to a place where those hands may be chopped off."

The Canada Border Services Agency disagreed and overturned the judge's ruling. In the summer of 2007, at the age of 26, Hussein Jilaow was flown on a private jet back to the country he hadn't seen since he was a boy. He had $300 hidden in his shoe, and he was well aware, since he had told others, that he was going to his death. By autumn, word had reached Canada that he had been killed. Meanwhile, deportation hearings were already scheduled for the other members of the Mad Cowz and the Africa Mafia.

"The interests of Canadian society outweigh Mr. Jilaow's presence in Canada and any minimal risk that he might incur if returned to Somalia," decided the Canada Border Services Agency.

That leaves us to wonder what the child version of Hussein Jilaow could have become had he received a little more intervention and help.

But before exploring how to save the fractured souls of children who have come from war-torn countries such as Somalia, Sudan and, more recently, Iraq, think back to that 11-year-old girl in Winnipeg's North End who daydreamed of a nicer neighbourhood. What will happen to her? How will that child be shaped by the violence she has seen?

The battlefield that may create tomorrow's gang members in Canada doesn't have to be in a foreign country any more. It has come to us.

Here's another question: What might have happened if Hussein Jilaow had maintained contact with his own child? Winnipeg police have literally seen a snapshot of one of those scenarios.

Imagine a photo of a young father smiling and laughing with a three-year-old boy in his lap—such a common scene, isn't it? Now put that father in gang colours. Then put his *toddler son* in gang colours. Now imagine that child holding a sawed-off shotgun. Winnipeg Police have seized such a photo in their investigations, and Staff Sergeant Rhyse Hanson says, "We were like, '*Wow*.'" His own personal point of view is summed up in a penetrating and simple question: *What chance does this kid have?*

How do you take that child and tell him everything he has learned from his parents is wrong? He has seen gangs become a generational scourge. "We're now perpetuating this, and so we have to come up with a solution that is beyond just the police or beyond just the community. We have to go right back to the root of whatever the problem is, find that root and try to correct it there."

~

To find those roots, they are trying to cultivate the garden right in downtown Winnipeg on Notre Dame Avenue at the NEEDS Centre. The acronym for the charity group stands for Newcomer Employment and Education Development Services. Refugee kids come from Somalia, Eritrea, Sudan and, more recently, Burma, where the military junta would like to wipe out one of the country's ethnic minorities, the Karen. They even come from exotic Bhutan. Some have never seen snow before—they step out of the airport into the unforgiving, skin-freezing cold and believe the white stuff on the ground is salt or sugar. For them and for their families, money will be an issue. Language is always an issue. Take a look some time at the unique circles of the Burmese language or the elegant symbols of Ethiopia's Amharic script, and then imagine you're 12 years old and trying to cope in Winnipeg. You can't even scribble a note to a stranger for directions as an alternative to using your few words of English. And within your first year of arrival, your family is likely to move four or five times as your parents try to find work, survive financially and integrate.

They call them "war-torn" countries, but those who work with refugee children have found rips and shreds in the psyches of these youths. These children have seen terrible things. They have lived in camps, gone without three proper meals a day for God knows how many days and suffered through family losses and traumas. But it is not easy to say they are desensitized to violence.

"I work with some of the kids who have more issues than adjusting to Canada, and I have to deal with them," says Heather Robertson, the Crime Prevention Program Coordinator and Psychosocial Educator for NEEDS. "And I had one kid say, 'I'm so angry. I just wish I was back in Africa so I could deal with this the African way—I could just take a rock and hit him in the head or something.' It's a different way with dealing with things, dealing with conflict, really."

Of course, picking up a rock or a gun is not really the "African way"—not at all. Because of their awful experiences, such kids have unconsciously accepted that violence is an inherent part of their culture.

"Exactly," says Robertson.

And she says these youths who come out of the war zones have never had the chance to develop problem-solving skills. "When there's a problem, they automatically go to one hundred in two seconds, and it's life or death. So they get angry, they just go. They don't have that ability to kind of say, 'Okay, what can I do to solve this problem?' Because back home you didn't have five minutes to talk over the issue."

She's quick to point out that while the issue of African youth in gangs has been highlighted in the media, it's not as if there is one "African" culture or these are casualties of one war-torn country. For instance, the Nigerian community, she says, has likely had more time to build a base and is therefore in a better position to help refugees coming over. Newer arrivals from Sudan, Sierra Leone or Burma have fewer of their own people established in Canada to call upon for assistance. Families inevitably move around in their first year, and "so it really just isn't conducive to integration."

In 2009, NEEDS received $1 million for its new LINK program, which will expand its services designed to prevent youth aged 12 to 18 from getting involved in gangs. It's expected to help 240 kids over three years.

Robertson says the centre has developed a kind of "mini-school" in the mornings for refugee families to help with their English and with their integration into the Canadian education system after they finally get permanent housing. In the afternoon, kids are told about the risks of gang involvement. They also get help with social skills, such as anger management and problem solving. She says many kids don't really know what a gang is or understand how recruitment works.

"For example, I was talking to one of my co-workers who arrived in Canada from Somalia when he was 16 by himself—he just came here by himself. And I was asking him, and he said—and this is a direct quote from him—'When I came to Canada, I hung out with members of the Mad Cowz all the time. They were giving me money, friendship and rides home.' He said nothing comes for free. Over time, they expect things from you."

It's an insidious process. Strangers who may come from the culture back home present themselves as friends, quick to offer tips and then money, maybe a gift like a bike. But then they might ask to sleep on the couch at a targeted kid's home or ask him to carry a package across a park. "And the next thing you know they're running drugs or they're involved in it, so sometimes it's not even a conscious decision. And the gangs are great [at recruiting]. They know where all the newcomer youth live in some of the transitional housing, and they'll sit in cars outside."

We watch them, said a former member of the Mad Cowz, if you remember. *Once it looks like they're ready, we go to them.*

To counter that influence, when a refugee youth moves out of temporary housing to a more permanent arrangement, NEEDS will pair a youth with a mentor for a year, because one of the most protective factors is a positive relationship with an adult. A mentor can introduce the youth to the different resources of the community, actually go with him so that he feels comfortable and safe. "So if that child moves four, five times in that year, they've always got that mentor, they've always got that one person who they have that connection with."

After all, Robertson points out, refugee youth might sit on a bus and come all the way in from the St. James district to the city core to use the centre's services, but he might stick around after the doors shut at eight o'clock at night. What then? He can be still at risk of recruitment while he's away from home and downtown at night. For a kid to be successful, the refugee family has to be successful, and considering that many of these fathers and mothers are often single parents coping with their own traumas and struggling with English, NEEDS also pairs some with family mentors as well.

Meanwhile, LINK program staff also work with schools to make sure refugee kids are being properly assessed and that their needs are being met. Their education may have been interrupted or they may not have had any education at all. These are children who arrive in Canada and, of course, must wait weeks before getting into the system. When they do, they can wind up in classes that are too advanced or too easy for them, with siblings of, say, 11 and 16 inappropriately in the same class.

Compound that with the fact that for many of these kids, there's been a drastic change in their role in the family—they once might have been a major means of support and now they're not of legal age to work in Canada. So the LINK program wants to deal with the low attachment to school and the frustrations of the youth before they become a problem.

For its recreational activities, says Robertson, it's important that they get members of the Winnipeg police force involved, even for something as simple as a game of soccer. Again, just as we saw in Calgary, there are kids who have come from nations where "serve and protect" has often been replaced by "abuse and indiscriminately arrest"—countries where cops were instruments of crackdown. Robertson says she once explained the Charter of Rights to some youth, including the provisions about having a right to legal counsel.

"And they were like, really?…So one of the huge, huge things we're trying to do with this one program is really break down that barrier, make youth feel police are there to help them."

One of her success stories is a 14-year-old boy from Afghanistan who had grown up in Iran because of the conflicts in his native land and who came to Canada in 2007. He had started working at a very young age. His father was dead. His mother was young and barely able to speak English. He studied English at a facility the kids took to calling the "Chicken Delight School" because it was close to a fast-food restaurant of the same name. He had extreme anger issues, and it wasn't long before he got beat up a couple of times by Aboriginal gang members. Four months after arriving, he was prime fodder for a gang of predominantly African members. The school allegedly couldn't or wouldn't do much.

"When you talk to him," says Robertson, "the main reason he joined a gang was he didn't feel safe."

The staff at NEEDS is still not sure just how involved the boy got, but he started coming to the centre around this same time. It sounds like they managed to reach him soon enough. "And actually now I wouldn't say he's one hundred percent, you know, 'this kid's going to be okay.' But he's no longer associated with those kids; he's working; he's going home at night. He definitely still has some severe anger issues, but I definitely think NEEDS Centre was able to give him that support he needed, and now he functions on a more positive level."

~

If the kids are lucky, there are resources within their small cultural communities as well. Then there's the matter of a community rediscovering itself when there's no clear ethnic tie.

In one Winnipeg neighbourhood, crime hasn't divided the people—it seems to have brought them together in a common cause, because there are those who don't want to wait to find out how gang violence will shape or hurt their children.

With gangs, drugs and prostitution, Point Douglas had become one of the most notorious problem areas of the North End. Then members of the community enlisted the help of their local cops. They started watching who came and went. They took down license plate numbers and posted them on a website. They even confronted criminal suspects, warning them that they were under neighbourhood surveillance. And this wasn't apparently just for crimes such as prostitution.

"Everything, whether it's prostitutes, the crack dealer down the street, or the body that turns up, people are coming out," says Staff Sergeant Rhyse Hanson. "They would go out there in groups, the citizens—organize themselves where they would take video cameras out and videotape things that were going on in their neighbourhood and even let the people know, 'We're going to turn this over to the police.' So it became well known that this type of thing was happening in the neighbourhood, and the bad guys decided, 'It's not worth my grief to go hang around this area, we'll just go somewhere else.'"

One of the leaders of the community effort was activist Sel Burrows, who wrote in an "op-ed" piece for the *Winnipeg Free Press* that residents save the police "for the heavy lifting." If guns or knives are involved, they'll depend on the officers. But "known gang members don't last very long in Point Douglas," wrote Burrows. "We had a bunch take over a small apartment block. The neighbours, white and Aboriginal, together decided they didn't like the illegal behaviour and started identifying what was going on. The landlord was contacted, and soon all of them were evicted. It took four weeks."

Hanson says the program worked phenomenally well and gives the lion's share of the credit to local residents. "Resources, when it comes to the police, are limited, and we can't be everywhere all the time. But the people in this community, they took it back, I guess for lack of a better term. They stood up and just said, We've had it, and they worked hard at it...."

The key, however, argues Hanson, is having everyone on board. "If you don't get that entire support of that neighbourhood, then no, you're not going to get the people coming forward, and it becomes a difficult thing to prove." He says that given the transient nature of the population in some neighbourhoods of the city—folks moving in, folks moving out and shifting around—it's difficult for people to take ownership of the problem.

But in Point Douglas, the tips and calls keep coming in, and the neighbours keep watching.

Chapter Six

"It's the Choices Our Sons Made"

Patti Bruneau is a talented country-and-blues singer in Winnipeg, a Métis woman who loves daisies, Tanya Tucker and family—though not necessarily in that order. She's also a parent who has wrestled with the issue of gangs, who has done the sleepless nights, wondering where her children are. Her son got involved in a gang, winding up first in Headingley Correctional Centre for aggravated assault and later in Manitoba's infamous Stony Mountain Penitentiary. One of her daughters also became a gang member. Bruneau's sister was murdered after she gave a lift to an acquaintance—she was killed as a collateral-damage victim when the gang shot their main target.

Once Patti went to visit her son at Stony Mountain, and as she sat and waited for him in the visitors' area, she noticed an older lady, crying hard and pitifully. As Bruneau wrote on a Facebook page, "I could see how much she loved this person she was visiting, whom I assumed had to be her son. I felt so sad for her, I wanted to just go give her a big hug and tell her that we'll get through this."

As names were called to see the prisoners, Bruneau realized that the sobbing woman was the mother of the man who had murdered her sister.

She says her "heart dropped," beating a mile a minute, and she began to shake. It was a moment, brief and fleeting, but it woke Bruneau up—because of her own grief, she had felt blame and rage towards her sister's killer and everybody who loved him and supported him. "It was like I hated them all." The two women looked at each other in silence, and Bruneau couldn't forget the woman's pain. "That's her son, that's her baby, that's her boy. And I just thought, you know what? It's not her fault, it's his choices—it's his fault; he made the choices, not her and not anybody else."

Patti's son beat the odds. He started his gang life at about 16 or 17 years old, but rather than wind up dead or constantly in and out of jail, he was actually *tossed out* by other members. Bruneau says the particular member he "was under" lost his own active status, which left her son at loose ends. Younger gangsters were coming up through the ranks, and they basically decided to thin the herd by telling him he was out—he had become a nobody in their eyes.

Bruneau agrees that these younger thugs probably did him a favour. "And I said to him that I was very proud of him because he could have fought to stay in. I'm so thankful that he chose to get out, and he's been doing great."

An ongoing concern remains for one of her daughters, who was recently involved with a gang.

The relationship between all mothers and daughters gets complicated during the teen years, but Bruneau says her daughter started acting out as young as 11—police brought her home after having found her in a stolen car. Having gone through a share of grief already over her son, she promptly told the officers to take her baby to jail. Naturally, they couldn't, given her age. It wasn't long before the girl was back in trouble. "Basically, they didn't do anything for a long time, and the law became a joke to her."

Bruneau tried grounding her daughter. She took away favourite DVDs, withdrew stereo privileges, tried different tactics. "And then I spanked her on the bum, and I left a bruise on her bum, and she went to school and told them I beat her, and Child and Family [Services] got involved, which I didn't mind—I'll take any help I can get. Because nobody was willing to help me. It was pretty much my fault."

At one point, Bruneau tried a scorched-earth policy in the battle because she says nothing else worked. The daughter threatened to kill herself, but apparently, the threats weren't enough for her to be placed in any facility.

Bruneau decided to lock her daughter in her room for a week with only a mattress and a desk, computer and phone cords cut, a key kept safely around the mother's neck. "I didn't know what else to do."

To Bruneau, the alternative was worse. On more than one occasion, she and her other daughter spent the night hunting for the troubled girl in filthy drug houses, looking for her child among the stoned-out ranks of the fallen.

Her daughter joined a gang where, ironically, the members apparently didn't care that she was a lesbian—but they expected her to "work harder to earn respect" and do more than the boys simply because she was a girl, the only one in the group. She was eventually busted for trafficking; she was holding crack cocaine, marijuana and the money from her drug sales at the time of her arrest. In 2009, Patti's daughter was released after serving a sentence in an Edmonton institution. Bruneau hadn't seen her in about a year and a half, though mother and daughter talked, and the daughter even wrote a contribution for a book Bruneau is working on about gangs and parents.

"I'm *hoping* she doesn't get back into it, but I mean, I don't know. I mean, I'm hoping and praying she doesn't, but it's ultimately her choice."

Bruneau is big on this point, on the matter of choices. She has never belonged to a gang herself, even though life gave her all the crosses to bear that could lead to trouble and the wrong roads. She grew up Métis in Winnipeg's Weston district in the 1970s, an era when bigotry against Aboriginals was open and tolerated. At the age of seven, she became a ward of the Children's Aid Society and was raised in foster homes, separated from her brothers and sister. But Bruneau ended up a working single mother. At the same time, she doesn't discount the deficits in the family equation of how it influenced her kids.

"I think now as I'm older and I think back on it, I was a single parent for most of their lives. Their fathers were non-existent. And I think maybe if their fathers would have been more involved in their lives, maybe they wouldn't be where they are."

Which is not to say she considers all of it her fault. "Once Child and Family got involved, they told my daughter that she had all the rights, and as a parent, I had none.... Everything went downhill from there."

Nor does she have a parent's predictable grudge against intervening authorities—Bruneau was a support worker herself for Child and Family Services with high-needs children. If she is bitter, it is over the apparent contradictions of a system that may at times serve those working in it far better than those who are at risk.

She says that when her daughter was acting out and a handful, "if she chooses to walk out my door at twelve o'clock at night or one o'clock in the morning, in order for me to stop her, I'm going to have to *physically* stop her." If she did, she says, she was at risk of being charged with child abuse.

"And then when I do let her walk out the door, and the police catch her on the street at three o'clock in the morning, the first thing they say is, 'It's the parents.' Well, you know what? My hands are tied, man. I don't know what to do."

She does, however, know what she would like to see done. Bruneau wants to see a stronger Youth Criminal Justice Act. She wants more programs that offer activities for young people, more intervention, more consultation between authorities and the communities. And it wouldn't be such a bad idea, either, to Bruneau, if there were safe houses where gang members could go when they recognize they need to get out. "Where can they hide? Where can they go to be safe where these guys aren't going to find them and shoot them?"

Meanwhile, she's started a support-group page on Facebook for parents of gang members, as well as her own talk show to discuss issues facing parents who have kids in gangs. She says it will air on the University of Winnipeg's popular radio station, CKUW-FM, starting out with pre-taped interviews but hopefully evolving into a call-in show.

And what if that forlorn, sobbing mother she ran into at Stony Mountain Penitentiary—the mother of her sister's murderer for whom she felt such empathy—phoned her show one day? "I've never thought about it, but if she did, I would definitely speak with her," replied Bruneau. "We're both moms, and you know, it's the choices our sons made."

～

There are more than the two solitudes of English and French in Canada. In the 1960s, '70s and '80s, to walk the streets of Winnipeg was to regularly see clusters of homeless Native men and women, often drunk, certainly malnourished, panhandling on street corners or sleeping on grates. Many died in the cold of neglect and exposure.

The notion of the aggressive Native man on the street was always a special fictional bogeyman for whites, but they could easily navigate past such spectres of urban poverty with just a look of brief—and completely useless—liberal pity. Gangs of any kind, certainly not gangs that included Aboriginal people, were not a serious problem 30 or 40 years ago in the city, if they existed at all. Turns out they did exist—only the two solitudes hardly ever collided.

Now they do. And Winnipeg has even more young Native men in gangs. So the question is: *What changed?*

One former gang member, James Lathlin, says that Aboriginal youth of his generation identified with poor blacks in American housing projects and ghetto neighbourhoods who were coming out with the first breakthrough rap albums. "Rap said, well, get a shotgun—to us a shotgun was to use in hunting. We'll saw it off and wear red, and you're considered a gang member, and you go do robberies and, you know, play the music....You know, instead of listening to New Kids on the Block, I'm listening to Ice T say kill a cop."

Staff Sergeant Rhyse Hanson of the Winnipeg Police says he knows of one Aboriginal community leader, who has now passed on, who was outraged by Native youth emulating black rap stars and gang leaders. Hanson didn't want to name the leader out of respect to his family, but says it used to upset the man terribly that some Aboriginal youth identified more with rap and American gang styles than with their own culture. Is it so simple? No one, of course, is saying that culture is the only factor, but it is one that plays a part.

Kathy Buddle, a cultural anthropologist and an associate professor at the University of Manitoba, is sceptical of the laundry list that often gets pulled out to explain youth gravitating towards gang membership: cultural breakdown, lack of a father figure, impoverishment, poor parental control, low school involvement....After all, the vast majority of Aboriginal people in Winnipeg live in poverty and may be single parents or come from such households. For many, there is a cultural break. But only a small minority of Native youth, just as it is a minority in every other ethnicity, wind up in gangs.

She underscores the fact that many Native youth have no sense of history over how their organization came into being. "And the police, who are involved with many of the kids who are dumb enough to get caught, also don't necessarily have much awareness of Aboriginal cultural traditions. So as a result, there's a tendency to want to look at things like media influence, media effects, as the causes of these sorts of behaviours when most social scientists will tell you that it doesn't matter how many violent movies a person watches....They have some influence, but by no means can they account for the phenomenon of the Aboriginal gang."

Buddle argues that it's important to keep in mind the historical context for when a gang is active. The reasons why a gang formed during say, the 1980s, might be very different than the reasons behind why a gang may form today. She's spoken to Native elders who identified themselves as some of the earliest gang members back in the 1960s. Back then, the notorious residential school system was still in place, with thousands of Aboriginal children forced to attend, whether their families wanted them to or not, while government-employed agents wielded enormous power.

One woman told Buddle how she was part of a group—two girls, three boys—that ran away and ended up in Winnipeg. Pooling their resources, they shoplifted and panhandled to survive, living on the streets. They dared not make contact with relatives in the city for fear that residential school officials would question their families and punish them if they weren't forthcoming about where their kids were.

"Even though there might have been Aboriginal gangs in the 1970s," says Buddle, "I think, to some extent, they were not anywhere near as visible as they are today." She believes that living standards and job opportunities have actually decreased for Aboriginal people living in urban areas. "Even though there's a great deal of criminal activity in some suburban areas, the big difference between the suburbs and the city is the suburban elites have the capacity and the funds to hide their crimes, while street kids and people living in severe forms of poverty can't. Everything is on the street, everything is visible."

She says that, increasingly, addiction issues are drawing many young Native men into gangs, not just in Winnipeg but across Canada. First they buy dope and get hooked, then they must join the gang to work off their debt. As the downward spiral continues, they almost become indentured servants.

Take Hobbema, southwest of Edmonton, where gang violence still claims victims (in 2008, for instance, a stray bullet from a drive-by shooting ripped through the wall of a house and wounded a two-year-old girl who was eating her Sunday dinner). A few years ago, when oil money was flowing freely, gangs targeted young Native men who stood to collect fat revenue cheques when they turned 18. The money was soon drained away from each one through drugs and debt. As with so many gangs, these ones preyed on their own community first.

Many of today's gangs with a high number of Native members are leaderless, doing the grunt work on the street for larger, more sophisticated gangs such as the Hells Angels. And Buddle sees female membership on the rise. For young Native women, gang life often begins when they become the girlfriend of a member, but girls may aspire to positions of influence they wouldn't normally have in the outside world or they may simply want to be one of the boys. The attractions of money and power know no gender.

Kathy Buddle may be a professor, but for her, the issue of Aboriginal people in gangs is not simply academic. Her former husband was Aboriginal; her daughter is Cree. She has four adopted children in her family, including a brother coerced to join a gang while in a maximum-security prison in British Columbia. Her adopted, younger Aboriginal sister suffers from severe effects of fetal alcohol syndrome and is on the streets. With few services available for troubled teens, the sister has been in and out of group homes, been addicted to crack and has worked as a prostitute for a gang. For the professor, the physical ravages and mental disabilities of fetal alcohol syndrome are not dry facts on a page; she has seen them first-hand.

"Now, if you take an average teenager who's already fairly impulsive and is not really prone to thinking about long-term consequences and multiply that exponentially, you have a situation where kids repeatedly put themselves into situations that are very risky and very dangerous, and then they don't really learn from the mistakes that they make."

As young as age 11, her sister made connections on the Internet and took off from school to meet these wonderful new strangers. She would often disappear for days—then the police would find her "living with five 35-year-old white guys who have been gang raping her for a week." Two days after being returned to a group home, the sister would be off again.

Buddle says kids with fetal alcohol syndrome or histories of severe abuse make perfect prey for gangsters because they'll do anything and don't really require anything in return. Like the increasing viciousness of gangs as a whole across Canada, this ruthless exploitation is a disturbing new trend for gangs that feed off Aboriginal communities.

She says another element may be socialization. Like that child in the photo holding the shotgun, many Native youth are drawn into gangs because their older brothers, their uncles, some family member is already in one, creating an image of normalcy. These youth may never get to see alternatives, only a life of easy money with no regular hours and without the challenges of an education system.

But she quickly adds that she's talked to people who are now youth workers who have matured out of gangs, who have seen media images of functional families to compensate for the corrosive glamour of gang portrayals and who have found other paths. "You know, they're saying, 'Okay, here are individuals who don't have to sell drugs, who don't have to share their girlfriends…who don't have to, you know, get out of bed at 4:00 AM every night to guard the booze can, who pursue a very different lifestyle.'"

As if the modern scourge of gangs wasn't bad enough for the Aboriginal community, sometimes the solutions lead to a new mess. Here is a story about that. It can be told different ways, but let's start with the version that made it into the newspapers and onto national television.

Back in 1997, Phil Fontaine was still Grand Chief in Manitoba, later to be elected to the top national chief position for the Assembly of First Nations. And he hired an unusual consultant for the issue of gangs—an actual gang leader, Brian Contois, the head of the Manitoba Warriors, who was paid a reported $2500 a month to offer his insights and advice.

The Manitoba Assembly soon reaped a whirlwind of criticism.

"Taking the tack that they did on it, I certainly feel that they're heading for disaster," Native Youth Councillor Curtis Fontaine told the CBC's Reg Sherren at the time. He was right. Contois was soon arrested on four charges of drug trafficking and wound up on the front pages of the local newspapers, being taken away in handcuffs. The man who gave him the new job, Phil Fontaine, claimed the arrest was a setup, but Contois was still quickly sacked.

Now, if you are outside the Aboriginal population, especially from a middle-class, white-bread background, the move looks, from a political standpoint, very much like a boneheaded play. Gangs are bad. Contois dealt drugs. Most drugs are bad. So, it wasn't either Contois's or Fontaine's finest hour. Even James Lathlin, a former gang member who speaks out against gang life to kids at schools and community centres, pours scorn on Contois. "He gave guys like me who are really actually doing the right thing a bad name. Like a meathead, he killed a good thing."

The tale goes that when Contois was arrested during the Assembly debacle, police officers were trying to figure out the best route to drive him to prison. "What's the quickest way to Stony Mountain?" one officer asked another.

From the backseat of the cruiser, Contois piped up, "Join a gang."

He was one of the founders and eventually the president of the Manitoba Warriors. The gang was originally formed, so the story goes, by those who wanted to protect the community from other gangs beating up individuals and preying on Native women. Their goal was to be a "warrior society," and the gang was even asked to handle security for Native band elections, watching ballot boxes and keeping things above board. Members didn't have to be the underprivileged clichés that fit neat boxes—some grew up on reserves and had come to Winnipeg for education and work and were fairly politically astute.

But the lifeblood of many an organization is coloured green, as in cash. The Manitoba Warriors drifted into drug sales and other criminal activity to raise capital. Still, they tried to follow a code—it wasn't the Ten Commandments, but there was apparently honour among thieves. They would never sell drugs to pregnant women. No Aboriginal women were allowed to be members of the gang. And even though they ran prostitution rings, they would not sell the sexual favours of their own women.

That all sounds ambitious and noble (relatively) until you start doing the cocaine, crack, pot and anything else you're supposed to be selling. The gang devolved rapidly as drug sellers became drug users, and soon all those great vows were ignored. It became impossible for the leadership to maintain discipline. What had begun as a kind of Native Guardian Angels had morphed into just another criminal gang, and the inevitable police arrests and stings followed.

Brian Contois has told others that he was never a drug user himself, though he did conduct drug transactions. According to Kathy Buddle, he was still a logical choice as a consultant when Fontaine wanted to tackle the gang problem. While he didn't look good to the mainstream media, or to certain politicians and even some other Aboriginal public figures, she says credibility is measured differently within the Native community. More weight is put on first-hand knowledge.

"If Phil Fontaine had gone to a social worker or to a non-Native police officer or to a priest to ask: Why are young Native kids becoming involved in gangs? In Aboriginal communities, that would have been considered to be second- or even third-hand, often heavily biased information by the organizations to which these people belong."

Critics suggested that by remaining in the gang, Contois tainted any useful information because a question mark hung over his motives.

But Kathy Buddle says that in stepping forward to offer information to Fontaine, Contois "really kind of sacrificed himself." One of the protective measures of the group against police had apparently always been never to identify the president of the organization. Contois was the top man. Around the time he went back to prison, he left the gang for good, which Buddle considers "pretty courageous" since this was a time when many Native youths were joining up, and he would need the gang's protection while behind bars.

"I think it was from the moment he denounced his membership in the gang that he sobered up," says Buddle. "And he didn't touch any alcohol at all and has been completely dry from that moment onward."

Contois has done some gang-awareness speaking engagements, but Buddle says he is still concerned about a possible price on his head or that gangsters might take him out for the sake of earning some glory. Worse, dangerous rumours have spread that he's a police informant—whether it's true or not doesn't matter, it's the kind of label that can get him shot.

That brings us to another irony. Individuals who get out and who might tell kids what it's *really* like, who can bridge that gulf of credibility, often put themselves at risk all over again.

～

"If you look at my body, it's a map to destruction," James Lathlin once told APTN, the Aboriginal Peoples Television Network.

These days, he spends much of his time as a gang-awareness speaker. He's not getting rich speaking to kids at schools or community centres, and when interviewed for this book, Lathlin was also working part-time in a group home, where he cooked meals, made up schedules and took kids on outings. But he has racked up some impressive endorsements with his cautionary tale.

Like many Aboriginal youths, Lathlin had obstacles to overcome in his early life. As his single mother struggled to make a life for herself in Winnipeg as a nurse's aid, having come from a reserve, young James was stealing cars, selling pot and then moving up the ladder of serious offences with breaking and entering and armed robbery.

Gang life had its attractions, especially when he was making $2000 to $3000 a day with people working for him as he organized socials on boat cruises along the Assiniboine River to launder his money. But he also succumbed to what he calls the "Tony Montana thing"—using his own sales product, cocaine. He wound up in the infamous Stony Mountain Penitentiary on drug and gun convictions. He had two years to think about his life and to write notes in a journal.

He says what straightened him out were his growing responsibilities. There was a woman in his life, bearing him a son, and he would have another son three years later. "My kids made me have a heart."

Now he offers his "Scared Straight" workshops to youth, describing his experiences, taking on the occasional smart-ass who doesn't buy his warnings. He says he will ask teachers or adults point blank if they are okay with the tactics he uses to get through to youngsters—tactics that can even involve taking down a kid who makes a violent challenge with a chokehold, or if the kid still isn't convinced, he'll ask "all the class to please stand up. So the whole class stands up. And I go, 'Now you have my whole gang mad at you because you have a big mouth. What are you going to do now?'" Lathlin says he's trying to drive home the point that gang life is one of ignorance, one of never thinking ahead or forward.

But he does have his critics. Another activist argues that Lathlin's core message of scaring the bejesus out of kids is misleading—it's not an absolute certainty that a gang member will wind up dead or in jail, and young children who hear one of Lathlin's talks could fear for an uncle or cousin because they're told with an adult's certainty that a favourite family member might die. As we've seen already, the chances are high for death, injury or jail, but some do manage to wake up on their own, move away from the life or get out another way. So the death-or-jail ultimatum could lose effectiveness, just as credibility died for the scare tactic that casual marijuana use will "always" lead to abuse of harder drugs.

However effective Lathlin's message may be, he has his supporters. One of them has been actor Adam Beach, best known for his roles in the Clint Eastwood–directed feature, *Flags of Our Fathers*, and the cop TV show, *Law & Order: Special Victims Unit*. In a video that's broadcast on YouTube, Beach, who has lived in Winnipeg's North End and West End neighbourhoods, says he himself got briefly lured into gang life. "The thing that kind of redirected me was becoming an actor. I found a volunteer theatre group for a lot of kids in the North End who were feeling troubled, and it helped us kind of explore who we were and what we ultimately wanted to be, because a lot of us just really didn't like ourselves."

Lathlin says he grew up with members of Beach's family in East Kildonan, and one night over dinner, he and the actor found out they knew some of the same people and, of course, had much in common as young Aboriginal men growing up in Winnipeg. "So it worked out nice."

Lathlin sounds more ambivalent about another endorsement. He got public support from Snoop Dogg, and it was thanks to the rapper's help that he got $5000 from the Tupac Ameru Shakur Foundation (founded by the mother of late rapper Tupac Shakur) to continue working on a book. "I'm sort of like, still thinking, he gave me money, okay, that's a good thing, and he told me that he wants to help people—like he has an inner-city football team, he gives money to churches that have community events. So he's out there putting in a lot of money, but at the same time he's doing a lot more harm than good, because the music that he's out there pushing is still talking about gangs."

When asked if he challenged Snoop Dogg over this, Lathlin says he did. Not that it was going to change the rap star's mind any time soon. But in debating the issue, Lathlin points out, "My kid listens to rap music every day, and I've said, 'There's a time to swear and a time to have a normal conversation. Between you and me, it's okay to talk a certain way, but when you're in public, you can't talk that way.' You got to show these people. You got to separate the facts."

In other words, distinguish between the image of the music and the reality. "You know when you look at me, like I come in with tattoos and the jewellery, and I say all these tattoos and jewellery was from my hard work. The point is, I didn't go rob somebody, I didn't sell crack to get this. I had a paycheque, and I went to go buy it. That's the same thing that Snoop or any other rapper does. You really try to break it down for them from the bad part."

Lathlin argues that celebrity endorsements—even from a questionable individual such as Snoop Dogg—has actually helped get his message heard. "When I come in there with Snoop Dogg and Adam Beach and Tupak [the foundation], well, it's a hands-down conversation. They'll sit there with their eyes on me, and that's it....So when I'm sitting there talking gang stuff—get a job, get a career, you know what I mean? They're like, 'Wow, he's right, working is cool.'"

In 2006, he was sitting with his children, watching a movie at home in his co-op block on West Broadway. He could hear a party for students going on in a conference room, and he says members of the B Side gang decided to "invite themselves." Lathlin says he heard yelling and arguing, and when he looked out a window and saw some young men by his car, he went downstairs to ask them politely to move.

Words turned into a scuffle, which turned into an all-out attack by 10 gang members. Lathlin was rushed to hospital with stab wounds, one near his heart and another near his spinal column. He suspects the attack was related to his work to deter kids from joining gangs. Certainly, it highlighted where Lathlin had failed to get through—a couple of his attackers had sat in on one of his workshops in 2004. As he told APTN in an interview, he had hoped his talking about his experiences would change the young men, or at least they would treat him with some respect.

Lathlin told APTN that the gang members turned on each other, helping Winnipeg officers make their case over his attack. "They're your friend at one point, but when it boils down and comes to going to jail or facing the consequence of your crime, they end up telling on you. So all that family unity and structure, 'We got your back'—it's not true."

If you recall, Calgary Police Staff Sergeant Gordon Eiriksson made exactly this point.

And there are other echoes of themes that we saw in Calgary. For instance, though Lathlin's boys might listen to rap music—a sinister bogeyman for some parents—he claims there's little risk of them following in his footsteps as a criminal. "Naw, naw," he insists. "They have a dad, and they have a mom, and they have the proper teachings. There's no way that could happen." His children are involved in activities such as boxing and a cadet program that can lead to police recruitment. "So their time schedules are pretty much packed."

~

When it comes to gangs and the Aboriginal community in Winnipeg, there is plenty of controversy over who wants to help and who may not have left the old life behind.

For six years, Paa Pii Wak, a halfway house on Maple Street in Point Douglas in Winnipeg, operated as a shelter for Aboriginal men trying to escape gang activity and drug and alcohol abuse. It was supposed to "promote, protect and support the physical, emotional, spiritual and mental well-being of Aboriginal males," while at the same time making sure recently released inmates kept to their bail conditions. It was the first of its kind in Canada, funded through all three tiers of government, and the media played it as a good-news story.

But in February 2009, Paa Pii Wak closed after a one-two combo of staggering blows. The first was a CBC investigation the previous month that discovered all was not right on Maple Street. For one thing, an ex-gang member had been running the joint for half a year without supervision of any kind, not even a board of directors. Then the Winnipeg police moved in, arresting several staff members and residents, claiming they had made the halfway house into a haven for gangs. The police alleged that several active gang members were employed, some of whom even supervised gang-affiliated prisoners sent to the halfway house. The charges included obstruction of justice for allegedly covering up for residents who broke curfew, drank alcohol and breached other bail conditions.

"The people who were recruited by the government to work there were not considered to be authoritative sources within the Aboriginal community," says Professor Buddle. "They were individuals who may have looked decent on paper, but people in the Native community were telling me all along that this was a place where recruitment was ongoing."

So to understand gang culture at all, one of the lessons may be to understand our own cultures first.

Professor Buddle has also warned in the past that some self-promoting gang-awareness speakers might actually be recruiting. "People tell you things, and over time, you learn about who has credibility and who doesn't," she explained to the CBC in 2006.

Rumours surround one activist over whether or not the person is actually out of the life. A source who doesn't wish to be identified claims to have seen the individual purchase crack cocaine in the Broadway area of Winnipeg.

There is a more disturbing story going around that at a drop-in centre, a recruitment attempt was made to get two boys, about 12 years old, to sell drugs. Staff Sergeant Rhyse Hanson, however, would not confirm or deny whether there was an investigation.

When asked about a witness seeing this person buy crack, the individual shot back, "Well, you know, I've seen you buy crack, too. I heard you were gay from one of the girls on Facebook. You know what I mean? It's all he said-she said."

The people who can afford to pay large amounts of money as clients, says the individual, have the resources to make checks. If there was any "funny business," this person insisted, it would have happened a long time ago. The individual mentioned there is a cousin of the same name who bears a close resemblance. In other words, it could be as simple as a case of mistaken identity.

At the moment, some leading figures within the Aboriginal community are distancing themselves and say privately that they will not work with this person, preferring to raise gang awareness their own way. Not all of this is related to the allegations; for some, it's also an issue of the activist's style, views and personality. Interestingly enough, this person says, "Aboriginals are my worst critics."

Only time will tell if there is something to the rumours or if this person is fighting the good fight and has been unfairly maligned.

"It's very easy to talk bad about someone, but it's very hard to actually compliment someone's work," insists the individual.

No ethnic community is ever completely unified in its political views. But at the moment, in Winnipeg, many of those trying to fight the gangs and erode their influence are also sometimes fighting among themselves.

Chapter Seven

"You Don't Do This, Then It's Going to Happen to You"

S hane didn't want to use an alias for his own protection, to avoid getting into trouble with any old associates or enemies. His first name would be fine, that would be enough. "I can't see many of these guys reading a book, you know what I mean?"

Shane is a soft-spoken, gentle Aboriginal man of 32, and listening to his laconic delivery without any boasting or effort to absolve himself, you wouldn't think this was a guy who once ran part of the Native Syndicate in Regina. Maybe that's it. The Shane who was willing to talk candidly about 15 years of gang life is not the same Shane who was once an ominous force in North Central. And when he spoke for *Gangs in Canada*, he had only been out of it for about 10 months.

In 2007, *Maclean's* dubbed Regina's North Central area "Canada's worst neighbourhood." In his profile of the district, Jonathan Gatehouse describes a Regina that would fit seamlessly into the bleak Baltimore of David Simon's television series, *The Wire*. It is a place where a man needs to keep mousetraps on top of his stove to combat the rodents trying to grab his meals, and where there are homes with no plumbing because addicts have torn out the copper pipes and sold them for drug cash.

"Corporal Ray Van Dusen, a community liaison officer with the Regina police," wrote Gatehouse in his article, "gestures toward a white house with the street number painted on red wooden hearts. The woman who lived there was recently evicted because she was running her six daughters—all under the age of 18—as prostitutes, he says. A couple of doors away, there's a little parkette. It used to have a jungle gym, but the city had to remove it—too many mothers were parking their kids there while they sought fixes or turned tricks in the wee hours of the morning."

This, in 2007, was North Central, the neighbourhood where Shane, a high-ranking member of the Native Syndicate, sold drugs and put women out. His background and his drift into the life is a cliché—too bad that some clichés are true. He says his parents were both severe alcoholics, and he was looking for family. All his friends were joining, and he really liked having a lot of friends, people who would look after him. He was about 18 years old when he joined the Native Syndicate. His initiation, he says, involved

stabbing a gang rival. "When I got recruited, the guy told
me, 'Okay, this is what you got to do to prove yourself.' He
told me, 'You don't do this, then it's going to happen to
you.'"

He sold a lot of drugs, mostly cocaine, and wound up
addicted himself. He ran girls on the street. Of course, there
was violence—armed robbery, shootings. "I was a crazy
individual that was down to do whatever. You could come
and say, 'Okay, we're going to rush this house and fuck these
guys up.' And I would be, 'Right on, let's do this.'"

Gang rivalry, says Shane, is mostly over who runs the
drugs in Regina's North Central neighbourhood and downtown core: Native Syndicate, NSK (Native Syndicate Killers), Redd Alert or Indian Posse. Wear the wrong colours at
your peril. For the Native Syndicate, the bandanna colour
of choice is white. "It can get really violent at times. You can
be just walking down the street and you can get severely
hurt or killed."

There is no one boss in the gangs of Regina, at least
not in the Native Syndicate. Instead, individual bosses run
crews of dozens of members. Shane rose to become one of
them, leading about 30 guys who dealt drugs and handled
the prostitutes. He says there were at least six or seven other
bosses with units of comparable size, and that was just for
one gang in the city of Regina.

He lived well. He had a nice apartment, cars, a woman
who loved him. His common-law wife, who has a normal

job, "knew what I was a part of, and she knew the risks that I was taking. Some girls want that kind of bad guy, you know? They like that little bit of danger, you know what I mean?"

But he says he made sure his children did not know what their father did for a living. And you *don't* sell out of your own home. "You had the house where you're living, and the houses in North Central where you sell from." In other words, you keep a low profile. Despite this, he still got hauled away for assaults and robberies, mostly for selling drugs. All those years…Did it maybe occur to him when he hit 30 that maybe he was getting a little long in the tooth, too old for the life?

"Yeah," laughs Shane, "but at that time, I was still pretty dedicated to Native Syndicate, and the thought crossed my mind, but the money was too great, too good to walk away."

Money like $5000 to $10,000 a day. As the crew boss, he naturally got a big slice of that, while his crew members would get smaller shares and the rest would go to higher-ups. The cocaine he used came from the quantity he was given to move, but he acknowledges that he might have kept more profit if he hadn't been using. Still, on any given day, he was walking around with a couple of thousand dollars in his pocket.

He is matter of fact about the mundane details of the life. How in recruiting girls, they had to have some kind of toughness, and they had to know how to fight. Did he ever learn where the drugs he moved came from? "Naw, I never asked questions like that....It wouldn't get me in trouble, but if I didn't know, then I couldn't say nothing, you know?"

What about the young girls he managed to recruit to sell themselves on the street? How do you even persuade a girl to do that? "Well, you get them hooked on drugs," he replies without missing a beat. "And then you take the drugs away from them, and you say, 'Okay, listen, this is not free no more.'" But don't they tell him off and leave? "Yes, they do," he says, "and when the addiction kicks in, they come back." It is that simple.

Shane seems the right person to ask about how gangsters feel, or whether they think at all, about hitting ordinary people by accident during drive-by shootings or assassination attempts on the street.

"No one really intends to hurt a civilian," says Shane. He says some people are just in the wrong place at the wrong time when the bullets are flying. But doesn't it ever enter the minds of these gangsters to hold off, to at least maybe wait until later? "No, as soon as possible, let's get it done now. If you would get to the place where it's going to happen, and you would say, 'Let's do this later,' you're going to make yourself look like you're a bitch."

Even if innocent people are around?

"Well, you know, it just happens, you know what I mean? You don't want yourself to be looking like a bitch, so you just kind of close your eyes and pull the trigger."

In the end, it wasn't a jail cell that took Shane away from the life—it was a hospital bed. One of his own crew was hankering for Shane's position. And he decided he'd get it by literally carving out the job for himself with his knife. Without warning, says Shane, his enemy walked in and began stabbing him. Shane was taken to hospital with wounds to his face, some of his fingers nearly chopped off and a near-fatal wound from the blade sinking in between his heart and his lung.

At first, after getting out of hospital, he was determined to get a gun and shoot his attacker. He didn't. He says the idea had always been in the back of his mind to escape the life, especially given that he once had to stab someone and had known it could always happen to him. And it did happen to him. So here was a chance for a final break. His common-law wife, the gal who originally loved the bad boy, had finally had her fill and was encouraging him to get out.

Once out of hospital, he visited his mother-in-law, who is a devout Christian, and wound up going to church. But even God wasn't enough. Yes, Shane had a bit of money stashed away, about $5000, but that didn't last long, and he was on the verge of going back to the gang even though he didn't want to. On a visit to a clinic for his addiction problems, he ran into one of his buddies, who handed him a card for Regina Anti-Gang Services (RAGS). After a few days of "bugging and phoning," he says the RAGS office finally accepted him into its program. When he walked into a program session, he found himself staring into the faces of young men he'd once recruited.

Shane now does volunteer work, and when he earns his driver's licence, he'll be taken on as full-time staff at the RAGS office. "Honestly, I'm actually really happy to be able to give back to my community for all these years of stuff that I was taking away from them. And it makes me really feel proud to be able to help these young guys not get into situations that I was in."

He occasionally runs into fellows from the old life, but they pretty much leave him alone because the word is out that he's no longer running a crew. "In the back of every gang member's mind there is what was in the back of my mind: 'I don't really want to be here, and how can I walk away from this without getting myself hurt or getting myself killed?' Some of them are happy for me because they are somewhat my friends. And then there are some of these young guys that still have things to prove within the gang, so they try and act like they're tough, bad guys, but when it comes down to it, everybody doesn't want to be in that kind of situation....So they act up for a little bit, but then they end up just walking away."

Plus he wasn't in a gang for 15 years without learning how to take care of himself. But he doesn't look for fights any more. He says he'll talk to the guys that want to talk to him so they know there's a better way.

~

The director of Regina Anti-Gang Services, the program that helped Shane find a way out, is Jacqui Wasacase. She's a funny, insightful, Jewish woman who married into Treaty status before the laws changed in the 1980s. On the Friday afternoon she was supposed to talk for this book, she had to reschedule the interview because she was busy escorting a 22-year-old female drug addict to a detox centre in Prince Albert with an undercover police officer. It wasn't safe for the girl in Regina. There was a hit out on her—when she got stoned, she had apparently talked too much and about the wrong things.

Wasacase's Friday afternoon sort of sums up, in a nutshell, what RAGS does. It's a self-referral intervention program, and you've got to want to be in it or go to its staff. A gang member might be looking for safety or need protection. Or the person might need counselling, life skills, court support, any number of reasons, but Wasacase says they mainly are looking for way to exit the life. RAGS is federally funded, but there is no halfway house, no bed facilities, just an office that runs 24/7. And if you're in a gang in Regina and in trouble, these are the people you likely want to call. Those that do call can be aged 12 to 30, but most fall within the heavily at risk early 20s.

"Every case is very different, and every case is very individualized," says Wasacase. "So we've had people who have given us a call at four o'clock in the morning because they've been shot at. And they've gone home, and they've freaked out, and they've thought to themselves, 'Holy shit, what am I doing here? I don't want this any more.' And so then we'll get that phone call. It can be a phone call where somebody has been charged for murder and has been sitting on remand for probably about six months. And here's our name, and he goes, 'Holy shit, maybe they can give me a hand.' Sometimes it's guys who are just wanting to talk. They don't really want to exit the gang yet, they just want to know that you're out there. We do a lot of support calls like that. We have guys that will come in because they are tired of it or they realize that, you know, they're getting older."

And they realize they've never held a proper job in their lives and might have only a grade nine education. But they want to make a change.

"We've had guys that have come in because their old ladies have said to them, you know, 'I don't want to stay with you until you get out of this shit.' We've had girls that have come in because they're tired of being beat up and tired of being on the streets. We've had girls that have come in because they've been charged with some pretty horrendous crimes, and they're taking the rap for their man. And then they suddenly realize they don't have to do that. There are so many different reasons."

Before RAGS, Wasacase was running a program called Transitions to Work, geared towards youth that were chronic offenders charged with auto theft. She noticed there were older guys looking at them as prime recruits. So she held a "pizza and Coke night" to talk to these kids about gangs. Wasacase believes they're the true experts—not the cops, not the academics, but the people you build a program around.

She says it took years to get the program off the ground, including her taking a research trip down to the South Los Angeles neighbourhood of Crenshaw, one of the hot spots of the 1992 riots, the place where they filmed *Boyz n the Hood*. It was the closest district she could find that matched certain demographic factors she was looking for, such as poverty and crime. When it's pointed out they might not be so welcoming of nice Jewish Canadian ladies in South LA, she laughs and replies, "I'm a bit of a chameleon." She can pass for Native, she can be Jewish, she can be whatever she has to be to do the work. "I would have made a great undercover cop!"

Now RAGS has eight "incredible" staff, and Wasacase says each understands part of that life. That doesn't mean they are necessarily former gang members, but they can empathize because they have survived addiction problems, family abuse, whatever. Wasacase admits that some who come to RAGS might still be conning themselves over their addiction or be involved in some ongoing criminal activity. But she says it's "Grand Central" in terms of information at RAGS, and staff keep an ear to the street.

"We're very good researchers, and the minute some-body comes into our program, we work really hard at uncovering everything we can about that person for their *own* protection and their *own* safety. The premise is when you come into this program you need to be honest....So if you're going to fuck around, this is probably not the program for you. If you're going to come in and be honest and answer all our questions, then we're going to be able to do whatever it is we can for you."

She says RAGS has a working protocol with Regina police and works fairly closely with officers, but not as any kind of information source for them, and the cops respect that. "So we have a fairly good working relationship with them. It didn't start out that way. I mean, you know there are, of course, lots of trust issues there, but I think over the last few years we've worked really hard, and they've worked really hard, and it's still a work in progress."

One of her success stories is a notorious gang leader who wanted to kill her. "You know, when somebody pulls a gun on you, that to me is usually a pretty good sign of a threat." But this is her community. And the bad-ass in front of her was a boy she had known since he was about 15. "Of course, in this job, the one thing you don't ever do is you don't ever show fear, and I'm not saying that just to sound cool, it's just—you just don't. So there was a certain amount of respect that was there between him and I, even if he hated my guts."

Fast forward to a year later, and the youth had been in jail, had gone into a treatment centre and had mentioned to a worker there that he felt he had burned all his bridges and had nowhere to turn. The worker phoned up Wasacase, who paid the young man a visit. "One of the things we chatted about—after he had apologized profusely," she says with a chuckle, "was the fact that he really wanted to make some changes in his life. And so he did."

He is now about 27. From cooling his heels in jail on charges of aggravated assault, he has gone through eight months of the RAGS program and will now sit in a university classroom.

Wasacase says you have to remember that "guys that become gang involved, they're not dumb or stupid by any stretch of the imagination. It takes a lot of skills to be a gang member, it takes a lot of brains to be a criminal. So the smarts are usually already there, and you can't discredit street smarts because those street smarts are what keep you alive. And it's all about transferable skills. If you are a really good drug dealer, and you are running 15, 16 guys on the street, you're running a lot of money....So a lot of it is taking those skills, those survival skills that are keeping you alive, and transferring them into something different in your life. And we all have the ability to do that."

Chapter Eight

Girls and Boys

They called her Big Jess. When the boys got into a fix or had a problem that needed muscle, it was "Get Jessie! Go get Jessie—she'll deal with it!" Oh, she was big all right—five foot ten by the time she was 16 years old. Big crazy punk rocker with big crazy hair and wearing a biker jacket. Of course, the look worked—we're talking mid-'80s here. And, hey, it was good for your crew to have a mean wall of Aboriginal chick who could go collect the money from the working girls, who could jack people up (i.e., mug them) or could give somebody a good stomping if it was needed.

No one ever asked Big Jess From Downtown to hook. Probably no one dared, but then probably no one thought of it, either. "I was one of the guys. There was no way I was going to go sell myself." Instead, she was an equal. One of the few—the *very* few—female members of a gang more than 20 years ago. She didn't come in as some guy's girlfriend or by selling her body as a pro. She was tough, and they knew it. She knew they knew it, and it gave her a big head, made her feel 10 feet tall.

Which is why she understands how girls get into gangs. And she's not an anomaly any more. Contrary to what's widely believed, a girl doesn't have to end up in a gang as someone's squeeze or by taking johns into a dark alley or into a room rented by the hour. There are some who do, like the adopted sister of Kathy Buddle. Then there are others like Patti Bruneau's daughter, who must prove how tough they are, just like Big Jess had to. Jessie McKay will tell you that today's girls in gangs are worse than she was. As one of the originals, she would know.

Big Jess is long gone. These days it's Jessie McKay— older, wiser, now a mature woman with a strikingly beautiful face, dark eyes and a light complexion, the punk hairdo long gone and replaced by tresses that flow past her shoulders. She has only been out of the gang life since 2002, but in a few short years, she has reinvented herself. That, in itself, is a minor miracle.

When it came to gang life, "I was pretty much born into it," says Jessie, echoing the idea about generations suggested by Staff Sergeant Rhyse Hanson of the Winnipeg police. Her mom, also named Jessie, was a tough broad with Scottish roots who ran with bikers. Most of her boyfriends were bikers, and if they weren't, they were truckers. Jessie says her childhood was punctuated by regular instances of packing up and moving in the middle of the night, as well as her mom going in and out of jail. By the time Jessie was in grade six, she had been in 18 different elementary schools.

Child and Family Services finally caught up with Mother Jessie and put her daughter into the foster care system. They gave Jessie back to her mother when she was 15. "And at this point, I hated her because she was the one who brought all this crap into my life, so I rebelled, and I rebelled hard." Already an alcoholic by age 14, Jessie needed a drink before she went to school—needed a drink to function at all.

In many ways, probably thanks to her mother's influence, Jessie McKay defied what was long a stereotype for Aboriginal women. Native girls used to be considered mostly docile, certainly no trouble. "They used to be very shy. Very shy, very timid—they wouldn't talk to anybody, wouldn't even look you in the eye. That was a big thing for years.... They'd keep their head down, they'd be very tightened up."

But her mother had groomed her, to put it bluntly, to be a hard-ass. "So when I saw my mom knock some guy's teeth out, I thought, okay, that's what I got to do."

McKay joined what she claims was the first real Aboriginal gang in Winnipeg, the Main Street Rattlers. She would party with members of their crew, hang out with them....Girls who joined became the "Rattlets." She later moved on to the Indian Posse, which got started around 1988.

"I just wanted to party, just wanted to fight. I was a big, hurt person." While she laid low when she was pregnant with her first daughter and later her second, even becoming a mother didn't push her to leave the life.

"It's the control, it's the rep, it's the rush—just knowing that you have all these people around you that want you." Until she realized, of course, that she was being used. But that took a while.

She wound up dating the chief of the Native Syndicate gang, who was eventually arrested for committing armed robberies. McKay was disgusted with how the gang started to fall apart after their leader went to jail. "These guys were fucking up left and right. They were drinking, they were just spending their money—they weren't putting the money back in for the guys who were locked up." Not for bail and not for lawyers' fees. She couldn't rely on them to raise any funds from drug transactions—money wasn't getting collected, and members weren't showing up when they were supposed to. But as the saying went, Jessie would deal with it. She stepped up. "I just had that mentality—I have to run the business, I don't give a fuck, I have to get this going, got to keep these guys out."

Her solution to help armed robbers was to commit more armed robberies. She hooked up with a proficient bank robber, and wearing a balaclava and a hoodie, she hit a branch of the Toronto Dominion on Corydon Street in Fort Rouge. She got caught. Jessie says the bell finally went off as she sat in a segregation unit of jail, realizing she could go to prison for 16 years over three armed robberies. It was only because she couldn't be identified in other jobs that her sentence was reduced to four years, which she served in Saskatchewan institutions.

She didn't want to hurt any one any more, but plenty of damage had already been done. Her daughters, who are finishing their teens as this book hits the shelves, "saw too much." She says there was no drinking or drugs around her girls, but they still witnessed the after-effects. They saw their mother's fists swollen from blows, saw "bitchy Mom," the mom who was hung-over for days, who couldn't find the will to take her children to the park, let alone hold down a job. Her eldest has been severely traumatized by episodes of domestic abuse between mother and father. "I fought him. I would fight him often....He was holding her in his arms one time [when the girl was three years old], and I was giving him shots to the head."

The little girl suffered horrible nightmares and acted out in ways much worse than just tantrums. "I didn't have the parenting skills. When I first had my daughters, I didn't know how to love them. I kind of looked at them like, 'Okay, now what?'"

Predictably, Child and Family Services took the girls away from her. Not so predictably, after McKay turned her life around, they let her have them back. Her youngest daughter "still has a hard time with it" and currently lives with her father, McKay's ex-partner. McKay says the girl has "forgiven her in her own way" and is doing extremely well, a straight-A student.

For her eldest, things are different. While never having gotten into trouble, "she's gone through every anxiety disorder you can imagine....She had a really rough end of it." McKay says her older girl could not get on a school bus or walk into   a classroom without suffering anxiety attacks, and by age 12 was already on medication and in therapy. But her daughter is an "awesome" artist, and McKay finally got her into a program for highly talented Aboriginal youth.

Her girls will not follow in her footsteps, but McKay warns that there are other young Aboriginal women who will, who are far more violent and ruthless than she and her peers were. "The young women that I know who are out there in these gangs, active gang members, they stop at nothing." Girls today are eager to show they can match the boys. "They want to outdo them. They want to make a name for themselves. They see how easy the money is from the guys, so they want to do it, too."

During the years when the stereotype was true that shy, introverted Native girls were almost invisible, cosmetic and clothing companies treated them as if they were. Few, if any, images of Aboriginal beauty existed in the mainstream media, and for the most part, that is still true. Is it any wonder then that some Aboriginal girls might want to outdo the boys when there is no model of femininity for them?

It wouldn't be a main cause for girls joining gangs, but McKay agrees it could be a factor.

More importantly, she sees the perpetuation of a vicious cycle—girls who see abuse, who suffer from a lack of education and who have no understanding of their own culture. "They don't know who they are."

 ∽

These days, McKay has been trying to keep other young men and women from falling into the gang lifestyle. She's worked as a coach and facilitator for the Circle of Courage program, which was organized by the Ka Ni Kanichihk organization in Winnipeg. Circle of Courage tries to help Aboriginal boys between the ages of 12 and 17 who are at risk. On its website, it says through "cultural knowledge and reclamation" that "young men will learn to become the 'warriors' that they were intended to be."

The program offers everything from one-on-one counselling and intervention to recreational activities like basketball to rite-of-passage ceremonies and other cultural practices. Culture is a big part of the program. But McKay says it's been difficult for Circle of Courage to hold on to male coaches and facilitators. Some are intimidated, others are frustrated by the challenges. One fellow who was hired for the job left after only two days, admitting, "I can't do this."

Jessie McKay could, and it's possible that "Big Jess" found a way to come back, albeit in a kinder, gentler form, this time to work for the forces of good. As the boys came in, often carrying their weapons—knives, eight balls wrapped in socks, bear spray—McKay took it in stride. "Me? My thing was, 'You know what, dudes, I know you need your shit to protect yourselves or whatever. Hand it in. At the end of the day, I'll give it back.'"

These young men often need basic life skills—how to open a bank account, how to get driver's licence, how to maintain a schedule for school and programs. McKay has also dealt with their families, because many of the boys have wound up in the care of their grandparents. "Every youth that walked in my door, I pretty much knew their family because I used to run with them or hang out with them or kick their ass."

More recently, she did crisis intervention work for Winnipeg's Macdonald Youth Services and helped work on a draft proposal to be sent to the federal government in 2010 on behalf of the Congress of Aboriginal Peoples. The Congress has its own National Gang Prevention Commission, and it will be looking for more than a million dollars in 2010 for a sweeping strategy to tackle the problem of gangs for Aboriginal peoples right across the country.

The scheme has to identify the needs of not only big cities, but also towns and reserves across Canada, identifying the gaps in services and how programs can be implemented. McKay says she was able to offer "tons of information, which is weird" because it's almost as if the government was finally catching up to her.

As an example of those gaps, she says, "We have nothing here in Winnipeg" for gang members past the age of 18—which is when the Circle of Courage program stops. "And as soon as you're 18, what? You've stopped? You're out of the gang? No, you're continuing, right, and that's the highest targeted age group, 18 to 30 [to be] active gang members."

As *Gangs in Canada* was being completed, McKay moved west to work as an outreach worker with Jacqui Wasacase's staff at Regina Anti-Gang Services, a job she describes as "awesome" and that she loves (but there's a twist to the story behind her move; more about that later).

McKay says her own brothers and cousins are still involved with gangs. She rarely sees them, but when she does, "I give them shit, I preach to them." She concedes that if someone had given her the same talking to at 25, she "would have given them the F-U."

So what can be done? "I hope they wake up, and I hope that they don't get killed. I don't know what else to do other than keep doing what I'm doing."

Chapter Nine

The Grim, the Good and the Guns

The two most notorious shootings of 2005 in Toronto happened after the "Summer of the Gun"—the summer was long over, but the guns were still going off. City residents were already astonished that 52 of what would eventually become 78 homicides that year would involve firearms, but the worst was to come during the holiday season. The incident that got the most headlines happened right after Christmas, and now they use the name of the victim for a shorthand reference. They call it the "Creba Shooting."

Jane Creba was a 15-year-old high school student who lived in the East End. She was a white, blonde, athletic girl, who was funny and who was like a "mother hen" in her protectiveness of her brother. Strolling along Yonge Street with her sister on Boxing Day 2005, she crossed over to the west side of Yonge near Dundas to use a washroom in a nearby pizza shop—and accidentally right into a crossfire. Two years later, the *Toronto Star* would report from a police affidavit that the fuse of the violence might have been lit 15 minutes earlier with a scuffle in the Eaton Centre between members of a North York gang who ran into members of a gang from Vaughan Street. It was believed that the shooting had started over as little as a dirty look. In the full-blown gunfight outside the Foot Locker on Yonge, six bystanders were hurt, with Jane Creba hit in the back by a single bullet. She died later in hospital.

By 2009, however, new facts emerged, and in late December of that year, Jeremiah Valentine, 27, pleaded guilty to second-degree murder and got life in prison. Valentine, who the judge said had a "predilection for illegal firearms," was carrying a loaded, snub-nosed .357 Magnum while he and a friend were shopping in the Foot Locker for a pair of shoes for his young son. According to the agreed statement of facts read out in court at his sentencing, Valentine's friend noticed another man come into the store hiding a gun inside his coat and giving them "penetrating" looks. Then they saw a large group gathering outside the store with the man. Valentine's lawyer claimed the group had surrounded Valentine and his pal, some of the men showing off the guns in their waistbands inside the store and demanding his gold chain, but these allegations weren't contested or included in the agreed-upon statement. When Valentine stepped outside the store, he challenged a man that he knew who was a member of the group, asking as he pulled out his revolver and waved it in the air, "Are these your boys? 'Cause these are my boys. And I have a .357."

When he pulled his gun, they pulled theirs. Mayhem. Chaos. Four to six guns are thought to have been used. The shootout lasted less than a minute, but these few loud and bloody seconds were enough to change lives and end one. Valentine fired his snub-nose until it was empty. According to the Crown, "While it is very likely that the bullet that killed Ms. Creba was fired from Mr. Valentine's firearm, that determination cannot be made with certainty."

Valentine has no chance of parole for 12 years. In reporting on the sentencing, the *National Post* said, "Contrary to long-standing beliefs that it was a gang dispute, the fatal shooting of Ms. Creba appears to have been sparked by no more than dirty looks and possibly an attempted robbery of a gold chain…" But this is still very much a gangs story. Valentine had 10 convictions for firearms, drug offences and failures to comply with court orders, and in September 2005, he turned informant, giving the police names and insights into gangs in the Jane-Finch area. After his interview, he signed an undertaking to appear in court over drug charges and was released from the police station.

"Some defence lawyers are questioning whether Valentine would have been released from custody had he not cooperated with police," reported the *Toronto Star*.

Police themselves now appear to have been conflicted over their gang source. The paper found one officer close to the circumstances who didn't want his name used but who argued, "A person has valuable information about a very serious crime, and without some flexibility many homicides would go unsolved." Valentine's information has been credited with the police being able to get wiretaps on the Driftwood Crips and charge more than 80 people in 2007.

But there was Valentine the source, and then there was Valentine the criminal. He was a fixture of downtown only because he had made enemies in the Driftwood neighbourhood. He mugged a victim at gunpoint in 2003, mere steps away from where Jane Creba and others would be shot near the Foot Locker. In 2004, one police officer wrote in a report that Valentine ought to stay locked up. "I'll say it again—this accused has a horrid, violent, dangerous, drug-filled record." When police suspected him in the Creba shooting, he was already in custody on firearm and drug charges.

With Valentine, it came back again and again to firearm and drug charges.

Guns and drugs.

Guns downtown, only because a criminal chose to switch his geography.

A little more than a month before Creba's death, there was already a public outcry over what was happening to

"Toronto the Good." On November 18, gangsters hit a brazen new low by showing up at the funeral of one of their victims at the Seventh Day Adventist Church near Finch and Albion in the Etobicoke district. The service was for 17-year-old Jamal Hemmings, murdered in a parking lot during another gang-related episode. His mother gave the eulogy. When close friend Amon Beckles—who was a witness to Hemmings being shot—stepped out of the church during the noon hour for a cigarette break, three gangsters followed him. They apparently waited for Beckles to pull the door open to enter the church, then one of them fired a semi-automatic handgun and killed him.

The 300 people at the funeral service dove for cover. "Everybody start falling to the ground," one witness told *CityNews*, while another described it as sounding "like something out of a Hollywood movie. It's the house of the Lord. I can't even—I can't imagine coming in with a weapon and discharging, killing someone."

This was the same church where a prayer march had been held earlier in the year over the wave of shootings plaguing the city. Irony is where you look for it, and one bitter postscript is that the shooting also happened while the city was running a gun amnesty, giving those with illegal weapons a chance to hand them in without fear of prosecution.

Creba's equally senseless death captured huge and prolonged coverage on the national news. Critics could make a case that reporters cared more about the death of a young, blonde, white girl than the murders of several black youths, but *where* Jane Creba died also had a lot to do with the media shock. As much as people in the rest of the country might think of Toronto as Canada's Sodom and as a potentially scary place, most of the violent crime until then had been confined to infamous neighbourhoods such as Jane-Finch or to suburban areas. Paul Bernardo was the *Scarborough* rapist.

Now a girl had died on Canada's most famous street and on Boxing Day, no less. Amon's mother, Nadia Beckles, actually visited Creba's school, Riverdale Collegiate, soon after the girl's death and told reporters, "Things got to change.... It doesn't look as though much justice is being done."

For the Creba shooting, arrests started literally minutes after it happened, with two suspects nabbed in the Castle Frank subway station. Four men charged with manslaughter were acquitted in late 2009, while Jorrell Simpson-Rowe was found guilty of second-degree murder and two counts of aggravated assault in 2008. The jury decided that he had fired a 9-mm handgun several times during the shootout and wounded three people. Just 17 when the Creba shooting occurred, Simpson-Rowe was sentenced as an adult in 2009 and will have to spend seven years in prison before he's eligible for parole. And as we go to press, two other defendants are still awaiting trial. On any given day, it's safe to walk along Yonge Street south of Bloor. For the most part, with a couple of exceptions, the headlines about gang crime went back to referring to districts outside the downtown core.

Meanwhile, justice still hasn't caught up with those who murdered Amon Beckles.

~

The York South–Weston district of Toronto had its own summer of the gun in 2009. For decades, the area that was most infamous for crime in the city had been Jane-Finch, but no longer. A police crackdown in Toronto's "bad neighbourhoods"—Jane-Finch, Rexdale, Lawrence Heights and Parkdale—apparently drove gangs into York South–Weston. This is where a youth centre keeps its doors locked around the clock so that only the kids who need its services can get in, and where residents have described an atmosphere of intimidation from the gangs in the neighbourhood.

Cops in 12 Division have long feared a "Jane Creba–type incident" in the neighbourhood, and in May 2009, they initially thought they had one. At a Weston high-rise block, a man fired two handguns into a family barbecue being held on the building's patio. A five-year-old girl was shot in the chest but amazingly survived. Superintendent Brody Smollet of 12 Division says the force expected public outrage.

"I was actually at work the night that happened," says Smollet. "And what I found unusual about that particular case was this—we believed there would be a big outcry over it because of the fact that she's five years old, a young, innocent child gets shot. You know what? There wasn't much of an outcry over that." Smollet chalks it up to the fact that the boyfriend of the child's mother, the man they believe was the intended victim, was an individual involved with gangs. "Because of her relationship to the mother and the intended victim, it just didn't create much of an outcry."

According to Josh Wingrove's feature for the *Globe and Mail* on the district's home-grown gang war, the little girl's shooting, as well as at least six homicides, all had to do with the fight for drug dominance between the Five Point Generalz, based near Lawrence-Weston, and the Gatorz of Woolner Avenue. Five Point Generalz wear "5PG" as either a shaved insignia in their hair or as a tattoo, while the Gatorz sport a simple "G," wearing green and Florida Gators clothing. As 2009 began, the two gangs engaged in tit-for-tat shootings that took them through the spring into the summer.

One of the shootings is believed to have been a case of mistaken identity, because 18-year-old Jarvis St. Remy had nothing to do with gangs. Jarvis had been watching TV up in his friend Courtney's apartment on Dundas St. West near Scarlett Road and was waiting for a bus. Jarvis' mother insisted that he be home by midnight, and he was calling his girlfriend when someone shot him twice. As Courtney was heading off to bed, he and his mother heard a bang, and she stepped out onto the balcony. She looked down and saw her son's friend lying on the ground. Rushing downstairs, she found Jarvis lying in a pool of his own blood. He later died in St. Michael's Hospital.

Jarvis' grandmother, Delores Wilson, told the *Toronto Star* that the family worried that as a young black man, Jarvis would be stereotyped as a gang member or someone caught up in drugs. "We are concerned that is what people may think of Jarvis, and of course, that is not true."

The truth is that Jarvis St. Remy wanted to be a computer engineer. He was supposed to graduate from high school soon.

As his mother, family and friends laid Jarvis to rest, they urged those responsible to be "man enough" to give themselves up. Instead, three weeks after Jarvis was shot, five-year-old Tanya Reynolds became the latest victim of the gang war.

Nor are the Gatorz and Five Point Generalz the only factions that have been preying on York South–Weston. There's the Trethewey Gangsta Killaz and Eglinton West Crips, while their enemies, the Bloods, operate in Jane-Finch and in Scarborough. It should be pointed out that Crips and Bloods in Canada have practically no affiliation or ties to the Los Angeles Crips and Bloods. Some experts suggest it may be a matter of local gangsters borrowing the famous names for "branding" purposes. A faction has also broken off from the Gatorz, and now the district must put up with the Southside Gatorz as well.

"It's a real odd mixture," says Smollet of the feuds in his division, "because sometimes they band together, sometimes they're at each other's throats, sometimes it's two against one, etcetera, etcetera."

But police began to push back hard in York South–Weston in the late summer of 2009. They rounded up some major players and slapped multiple charges on them over drug trafficking and threatening death. (The charges are working their way through the courts as we go to press; one of the alleged top gangsters was already in the midst of appealing his deportation back to Jamaica over his criminal behaviour—a previous deportation ruling had been quashed in 2004 because a panellist on the Immigration and Refugee Board argued he was "more than unlikely to re-offend.") And in late June, 32 TAVIS (Toronto Anti-Violence Intervention Strategy) officers joined 12 Division for a short stint. The controversy over not enough being done turned into *how long* the job would take to do. Residents of York South–Weston knew the extra cops in the neighbourhood would eventually pack up and be deployed elsewhere. "Give it three weeks after that, the community will be back the way it was," predicted one resident.

It's an outcome that even Superintendent Brody Smollet conceded was possible when he spoke to the *Globe and Mail*. "What we're doing right now could simply be sticking your finger in the dike. And the instant these officers leave, it could all start up again. We really don't know. We don't like to think that could happen."

But a couple of months later, when speaking for *Gangs in Canada*, the superintendent was more positive. True, half of the extra officers left halfway through September 2009 and the other half were gone by the end of October. But Smollet claimed there was a lot still going on behind the scenes. "We've identified pretty much every gang member that's in the division, and even some of the wannabes. And we're targeting them, we're putting pressure on them, we are questioning them all the time."

Smollet even credited the local community groups with occasionally offering good leads. They come up with "interesting information"—not always accurate information, of course, but they apparently offer tips the police can use to at least investigate.

And the police, promised Smollet, are quite aware that some of the problems plaguing the neighbourhood might have been "displaced" while York South–Weston enjoyed the respite of extra officers...and those problems just might find their way back. But they have a plan. It's one that involves many other units from across the force. No, he couldn't go into the details, but "We are hopeful that that plan will keep a lid on things..."

Time, of course, as they say, will tell. For York South–Weston, the tragedy would be if things go back to the way they were that summer. The tragedy for Toronto might be that gang crime never really stops, that perhaps it simply moves on to a new neighbourhood, until the bloody circle is completed and the migration starts all over again. Time will tell over that concern as well.

~

In those old black-and-white movies and TV shows about juvenile delinquency—you know the ones, where the kids all have neatly trimmed hair and look closer to 30 than 17, just like more recent "teenagers" on *Beverly Hills, 90210*—they often referred to "zip guns." And you might well wonder: what's a zip gun? Turns out it was an improvised firearm. For the gun barrel, you used the tube rod of a coffee percolator or a broken-off car antenna, taped it to a block of wood for a grip and then rigged up a rubber band with a firing-pin mechanism to launch a .22-calibre bullet. The problem with such a jerry-rigged piece of mayhem was that it was inaccurate, risking hurting or killing bystanders, and could blow up right in the shooter's hand, causing him to lose fingers.

The zip gun wasn't a weapon they used out in the sticks; it was popular in Brooklyn and Queens, too. Juvenile offenders still broke into American gun shops in the 1950s and '60s to steal properly manufactured weapons, but it's interesting that youth of that era resorted to a deranged shop-class method to make guns.

What does that have to do with gun crime today? After all, young people today don't bother to MacGyver a firearm. They don't have to. But once upon a time, it was *harder* to get one. There might always have been the impetuous little sociopath with a chainsaw smile who would go ahead and rig a zip gun, but there might also have been two or three salvageable boys who thought twice over a pal who lost most of his digits after his zip gun exploded in his hand.

Time to discuss the real thing. The truth is that most of the guns causing destruction and tragedy on our streets come in from the United States. A study published in 2009 for the *Journal of Criminology and Criminal Justice* reported that two-thirds of crime guns seized in our country come from south of the border. It should be noted that one of the study's authors, Wendy Cukier of Ryerson University, is a gun-control advocate, but she was not the only author. If you don't like those numbers, consider that in 2006, the Toronto police managed to trace back 120 out of 181 guns used in crimes in that city to the U.S. In 2009, of the 510 crime-related firearms in Toronto seized during the year up to late September, only about 30 percent were stolen locally, with the rest smuggled into Canada.

And so we come to Audette Shephard, who is the chair and president of UMOVE, United Mothers Opposing Violence Everywhere. Shephard is a youthful, articulate woman, a devout Seventh Day Adventist who came from Trinidad and who worked her way up to be a manager in global transactional banking. She is also the mother of a teenager who was pointlessly gunned down in Canada's largest city.

It's important to underscore here that her 19-year-old son—like Jarvis St. Remy, like Jane Creba, like Keni Su'a in

Calgary, like Phil Haiart in Winnipeg and on the list goes—
was not involved in any gang activity whatsoever. And his
death seemed to have nothing to do with gangs. It's still not
clear what the issue was behind his murder, not that any
grudge would justify it to those who loved him or make the
loss any more bearable. But for Audette Shephard, her son's
death has a lot to do with the issue of guns on the street—
and with other issues that relate to the gang problem in
Canada.

Her son, Justin, was a talented basketball player, talented enough that he was on his way to the University of
Maryland on a full scholarship. His dream was to play one
day in the NBA, where he'd already have family company—
his half-brother is Jamaal MaGloire, a pro player for the
Miami Heat. Shephard says one of MaGloire's friends was
so impressed with Justin's skills that he told Jamal, "You
better watch it—your little brother's going to come and eat
your food."

Mother and son were close. Justin got a tattoo of
her name on his chest. Shephard thought he might put
a girl's name on his body, but Justin replied that there was
no one else he loved more than his mom. They had moved
recently from Mississauga to the Parliament and Sherbourne
area so both could use the subway for easy trips to his school
and to her work. At one time, she knew all her son's friends,
but when they moved, that changed, and she suspected that
some of the new faces hanging around her son, who was
a trusting young man, simply wanted to be close to a rising

talent. "When we were downtown, I told Justin, 'Some of these guys, they look kind of shady.'"

"Mom, you always like to judge," he replied.

But she didn't have a good feeling about two of them, especially after instances when she would come home, and they would quickly leave. Her son would tease her, "Mom, you're a stalker. Stop stalking me."

On June 22, 2001, late at night, someone called Justin at home, and he told his mother he would be back in 10 minutes. He left and never returned. Around one o'clock on that Sunday morning, he was found dead on the Rosedale footbridge, shot twice in the head. About that same time, a car was seen speeding south on Glen Road, and it slowed down as it approached the entrance to the footbridge. A man was seen running from the bridge into the car, which then sped off.

To this day, Justin's killer hasn't been found. There are those who might know things, but they're not talking. She spoke to the mother of one of the individuals, who told her she wanted her son to speak out. But the next day, a lawyer apparently called one of the detectives working the case and reported that his client wasn't interested in talking after all.

"So I have no idea why a 19-year-old is a client in a situation like this," says Shephard.

She says the two detectives who originally worked the case have moved on, and if there's any new break in her son's murder, other staff will inform her. Quite honestly, she has no more expectations from the police. "I just rest on my faith that that person will face their justice. They *will* be accountable for their actions. Doesn't matter if I don't see them go to jail—they *will* be held accountable. I believe it a hundred percent."

Instead, she has focussed her energies into UMOVE, which has a small core membership of 15 parents who have each lost a child to violence. Small, yes, but the group has made itself heard in the media and has gotten the support of key politicians. When Shephard spoke for *Gangs in Canada*, UMOVE was still organizing a drive to send 5000 post-cards—every postcard carrying a photo of a young murder victim—to Prime Minister Stephen Harper for the group's call on a full ban on handguns.

"You never hear about a drive-by stabbing or a drive-by baseball batting or anything like that."

Her son, Justin, she argues, was a big, strong, athletic teenager who would have had better odds of survival if he had faced, say, a knife or a baseball bat. She's not wrong. In martial arts dojos and self-defence classes, students are regularly taught how to counter weapons such as a club or a knife, but these tactics are for use only if you cannot escape. The best defence against a knife or a club is to *run*. Run like hell if you can. That doesn't work well with a gun.

And Shephard is withering when it comes to the issue of gun culture. "You know this gangster thing is so glorified and glamorized that every little thug on the street, every little punk on the street wants to be 'packing,' wants to walk with a gun. So the gun seems to be what gives them the power, because some of those guys, if they were to face a conflict without a gun, they would *not* be there."

She doubts that half of them would be running off to pick up alternative weapons if the guns weren't readily available.

For her, a gun is a "weapon of mass destruction." It's true that a gun is a most democratic weapon, one that requires little skill or even thought to use, made convenient by manufacturers the same way appliances are. You pull the trigger. Its lethal purpose relies less on proximity than a knife or a club, so the personal aspect gets taken out of it. Unless someone's shooting back, you don't risk getting hurt by your victim defending himself. If you want to stab someone or bash his brains in, even if it's from behind, you have to get close, and there is still a risk to yourself—and you must still be close to what you did afterwards. It can be *very* personal. Not so with a gun. Pull the trigger metres away and stop caring.

"I go and talk in schools to youth," says Shephard. "I go to Woodbridge, I go to Vaughn, I go to Regent Park, I go to Victoria Park, in different neighbourhoods, and all through the message is the same—it's very easy to get a gun."

She has heard the arguments of gun owners and is unimpressed—how guns don't kill people, people kill people, how there are law-abiding, target-shooting enthusiasts. She argues that society can't depend on such gun owners crossing their fingers for us that their weapon may not be stolen some time in the future. Eliminate the possibility of the theft of a deadly weapon by not allowing anyone to have it in the first place.

"I guarantee you, the boys using those guns are not the ones bringing them through the border. There are gun traffickers who are making millions of dollars on the deaths of our kids by supplying the guns."

She says that Canadians have to start looking hard at themselves, too, since we have our own share of companies that manufacture guns, like Para-Ordnance, and that make ammunition right here at home. And she says Chris Rock had a point with an insightful joke. "You don't need no gun control, you need bullet control!" argued the comedian. "We need to control the bullets! I think all bullets should cost $5000. You know why? Because if a bullet cost $5000, there'd be no more innocent bystanders!"

Shephard is also well aware that a gun ban isn't enough to address the social ills and cultural disconnects that can drive young people to pick up a weapon in the first place. She says when she talks to school kids, she tells them they can be empowered to make the right choices, to take the staircase one step at the time, and that life isn't all about the "bling," about getting rich quickly. The bar has been raised since she went into banking in 1974. While some kids "think their parents are trying to curb their fun or cage them up," we need to make them understand that we have the examples of our experience.

She's concerned with values and says the school curriculum needs to include character development. Many might part company with her when she talks about what, for her, is a "burning issue" over prayer in schools, but she says it's not about traditional religion or telling anyone how to live their lives, but about the relationship you have with the Creator. Many would still put Audette Shephard on the side of the angels for her fight to keep deadly weapons out of the hands of violent kids and violent people altogether.

Some, of course, will insist that a gun ban "isn't enough to stop the violence." No one, including Shephard, is claiming it will be.

But she would probably argue that it's a good start.

❧

Kids tell Audette Shephard it's easy to get a gun. Toronto Police Staff Sergeant Sharon Davis will tell you something else. She's in charge of the force's School Resource Officer program, which places individual officers in specific schools so they can build relationships and a degree of trust with teachers and students.

Davis says it's still pretty hard to get a gun if you're a young person—unless you're in the right place, at the right time and with the right connections. In fact, she insists, any kind of weapon in a Toronto school is a "very, very rare event." She says that in 2008, only one gun was seized on school property. "Toronto schools are overwhelmingly safe places to be. Surveys show young people feel safer in their school than they feel any place else in the community."

Maybe kids do feel safe at most Toronto schools, and maybe there aren't that many weapons in most of them. Unfortunately, that hasn't been true recently of C.W. Jefferys Collegiate in Toronto's notorious Jane-Finch area, where in 2007, 15-year-old Jordan Manners excused himself from a class to go to the washroom and ended up shot dead on the floor. Later, there was a stabbing at the school. After the death of Manners, a three-member panel led by lawyer Julian Falconer probed school safety and spoke to dozens of teens over the course of months.

The Falconer Report is a brick of 1000 pages that relates in horrifying detail everything from a recap of the Manners shooting to a Muslim girl being sexually assaulted by six males in a school washroom. Some black students claimed, "It's easier to get a gun than a job."

When Falconer released his final report, he told a news conference in January 2008, "The truth is there are guns in our schools in non-trivial numbers across the city, and neither the police or the [Toronto District School Board] are in the position to track guns at any given school." And as far as other weapons go, Falconer suggested, "You could fill a Home Hardware with the amount of knives kids bring to school, but we don't find them."

And if surveys show most Toronto schools are "overwhelmingly safe places" as Davis argues, it sure wasn't true of Westview Centennial Secondary School in 2007 and 2008. As the *Globe and Mail* reported, "one of every five students felt unsafe at school; 40 percent reported they had been threatened with physical harm, 15 percent with a weapon; many admitted seeing guns and knives in the school—20 students even admitted bringing a gun to school—and as alarming as any of that, fully 80 percent of student respondents at both Westview and Jefferys said they wouldn't report a crime, even against themselves, to either police or school officials."

And here's the irony. The School Resource Officer (SRO) program has encountered resistance at the very schools in the Jane-Finch area where it might be most needed, Jefferys and Westview. If staff at the schools wanted SROs, some parents and students apparently didn't. As the new school year began in 2009, the flag for the "Against" side was raised by the co-chair of Westview school's parent council, the improbably named Reverend Sky Starr. Starr claimed that kids simply didn't trust the cops and that one of the big issues for students was that the SROs would be in uniform and armed.

"We're not saying no" flatly to the SRO idea, according to Starr, "but it shouldn't be a one-size-fits-all program."

If Westview and Jefferys have been uncertain about taking SROs, there are plenty of other schools that want them. The program was expanded to 50 schools in 2009, and more schools want officers than the force can provide.

All the issues of trust in the police, of whether hallway lockers are full of weapons or not, do relate to gangs when you wonder if kids feel so at risk that they might organize themselves into such groups for self-protection or could be easily swayed into joining one. Davis flatly insists Toronto schools aren't recruitment centres for gangs in the way that they might be elsewhere in the country, "because the ones that would be most active in a gang simply aren't going to school. They're supposed to be, but they're not."

The issues faced in places like Surrey, Regina and Winnipeg are "very different than ours, because we're in a somewhat privileged position that we've got a good enough handle on most of the violent crime in the city, that we've got the time where we can give some of it to engagement and interaction. We can partner with people. Because police are not your main social development mechanism. Police can't, you know, provide better parenting. But we are in the position where sometimes we can get involved in social-development activities, and that makes a difference." But Davis says not to forget that the other part of the job for officers is enforcement. "They do make arrests."

A number of replica weapons were recently seized, she says, but in every case it was a situation of a young person who was being bullied. No gangs were involved, nothing like that. In each case, the tormented youth thought he or she could demonstrate power and control by bringing the replica to school. "A lot of those weapons and drugs seized and prevented were because young people came and told the [school resource] officer, who took appropriate steps."

This is interesting. Not only because of the contrast in attitudes and perceptions at Westview and Jefferys, but because of what has been going on in the United States with the "stop snitching" culture. The term "snitch," of course, once referred and sometimes still does to someone who is actually involved in a crime and informs on his or her pals. But those who push the "stop snitching" doctrine in some underprivileged city neighbourhoods of the U.S.—prime turf for gangs to prey on—want to extend that to innocent non-combatants who just want to live their lives and get by. It's a disturbing concept in its implications to say the least, the idea that ordinary residents should be made to feel they've betrayed criminals simply because they look for help from the authorities—it's intimidation wearing a varnish of counterfeit honour. And from Los Angeles to Pittsburgh, there have even been "Stop Snitching" T-shirts sold.

So in Toronto, the surprise isn't that kids sometimes don't talk, following the code of the street, but that they sometimes will.

"We have that here, too," says Davis, "but there's a difference between snitching in the context of 'Something has happened, I have no idea who these people in uniform or suits are, I want nothing to do with it,' and 'I know Officer Ron. I trust him. I like him, and I want to protect somebody.'"

What about kids who are troubled and at risk? Davis points out that "there are new rules in the Education Act. You just can't kick kids out of school anymore. Not getting an education, technically, is not an option in Ontario. One way or another, even if we are going to expel you, we've got to come up with an education plan. And there are a lot of really interesting things going on in Toronto to help with that."

Davis cites the Pathways to Education Program created by the Regent Park Community Centre. According to its website, over eight years, the program has increased college and university enrolment of Regent Park graduates from 20 percent to 80 percent while cutting absenteeism by half. And as for the kid who does get expelled from one school and integrated into another, a school resource officer can be there when that young person gets orientation to his new alma mater.

"So one of the first people they meet is a cop, which gives an indication of whatever it was that caused you to be transferred to this school from your other school: 'I now know you, and I'm watching you.' But the other part of it is because of the skills these officers bring to the job: 'I'm also here for you. And if you want to be pointed in some good directions, this is a fresh start. Let me help you.'"

It's not a case of the officer helping the kids with their homework every night. But one of those good directions, says Davis, is a school's Empowered Student Partnerships Committee, in which students themselves design programs and activities to address safety issues. Those can be anything from graffiti to iPods being stolen to sexual harassment in the hallways.

Which brings us back to the divide between the cops and the kids at Westview and Jefferys Collegiate. "In few other parts of the city is the chasm between police and those they police so big," reporter Christie Blatchford wrote for the *Globe and Mail*. If the chasm doesn't somehow get bridged, if kids at school don't trust police over weapons or incidents of violence and sexual assault, it isn't difficult to imagine they will carry these attitudes with them as they become older members of the community. So even if gangs or recruiting aren't a major problem at many Toronto schools, as Davis says, the School Resource Officer program might be seen as one preventative measure.

"Police are not in charge of fixing the gang problem," says Davis bluntly. "Gangs are a social issue, and if it's gotten to us, it's gone too far. Police are not the first line of defence in gang prevention."

~

Every little punk on the street wants to be packing...

In the theatre production *Diss*, the up-and-coming gangster Tyrone is downright high after he pulls his gun on a clothing store salesman. What was intended to be a fun jacking of clothes—shoplifting T-shirts and jeans while the staff person is distracted—turns ugly fast. And in the aftermath, Tyrone is juiced with adrenaline from his quick moment of power. He's ecstatic.

"Did you see that guy?" he asks. "He was going to piss his pants. Man, I loved that. I loved that. I shoulda got everybody in the store down on the floor. Hey, get down—get down or I'm gonna blow your friggin' brains out—down—right now. Pow! Pow! Pow! Right?"

"Yeah, sure," replies his pal, Jesse.

"Right," mutters the most recent gang recruit, Sammy. For it's starting to sink in, the enormity of what they've done, the storm into which they've steered their young lives.

The play features a generous portion of rap and slang that is likely quite fresh in terms of what's used on the street these days. No surprise, since several young people—including gang members and youth at risk—consulted on the play and contributed raps and dialogue to playwright Rex Deverell's script. With the media oversaturated with hip-hop culture, it's easy to become impatient with its use as a storytelling crutch or even as a means to connect with a youth audience. But *Diss* includes refreshing moments in which the audience can feel the authenticity of the crisis.

"Let me spell it out for you," Jessie tells Tyrone, and any slang or street rep persona quickly falls away. "You just took us from ripping off a store to armed robbery."

It's certainly not the first time someone thought of using the arts to reach kids over the gang issue. A 40-year-old Catholic high school teacher consulted with Peel Regional Police to write and direct *Mouse*, a 20-minute video about a 10-year-old boy lured into the gang lifestyle. It wasn't hard for the film to draw on real life—about a dozen of the murders in the Peel region in 2008 reportedly took place in an area around the school, and most of them were supposedly drug and gang related. *Mouse* is a cautionary tale that ends with the protagonist sitting in the back of a police cruiser while his helpless mother tries to touch him through the window. The teacher-author told the *Catholic Register* that the character named JP—as opposed to JC, which he said would be "too obvious"—is a Christ-like figure, despite still being a gangster. The ReelWorld Film Festival gave *Mouse* an award as Best Canadian Short Film, quite possibly more for its good intentions than it being powerful art.

Diss doesn't offer a Christ-like sacrifice or even a moral as in a heavy-handed after-school special. The death that happens in the narrative is sudden and senseless. Unlike the arrest in the short movie, the play ends with Sammy taking a criminal action that is sure to be a disaster. But we will never actually know what happens to him.

The play is a product of Mixed Company Theatre, which runs out of a pleasant office on the second floor of an old church on Toronto's Carlton Street. Walk past the old Maple Leaf Gardens away from the safe bustle of downtown, past Jarvis where hookers often shake their wares at night, and you find yourself in a peculiar no-man's land of shabby retail shops and apartment block complexes before you reach the gentrified cheer of Cabbagetown. Walk south of Gerard, and you find yourself in what the *Toronto Star* calls the most violent quarter of the city. It's somehow appropriate that Mixed Company is located here, given that it often deals with individuals whom society forgets.

What's possibly most interesting about Mixed Company's effort—something that didn't get much press—was how it put on a show first for a captive audience of highly sceptical Toronto cops. There was apparent controversy in 2008 over how the Toronto Anti-Violence Intervention Strategy (TAVIS) was dealing with youth.

The story goes that an officer would go up to someone, and it would all be very polite with how are you, what's your name, can you show me some ID? And then an hour later, another officer would make his or her way through the area and start the drill over again: How are you today? Live in this area? And on and on. It would be easy enough for a teenager to feel targeted or harassed. TAVIS realized it could do better and worked with Mixed Company to create a short theatrical piece that presented different scenarios so officers could "rehearse for reality" as artistic director Simon Malbogat puts it.

One might think a bunch of cops would react with a certain degree of hostility and cynicism as they were made to watch what they probably expected to be touchy-feely theatre. "They did," admits Malbogat. "But what we did was surprise them. Because they loved it....We show the worst-case scenarios so that we catalyze an audience to want to change, to want to do it differently. So we have police officers who said stop, because what we showed was a police officer who didn't do what was conducive for the community. So they stop, they come down and they show the other police officers how they would deal with this youth and make it much more within a positive aspect..."

Welcome to what Malbogat and associate artist Duncan McCallum call "forum theatre," the kind of live theatre that has a "press pause" during which audience members can put in their two cents and act out alternatives. McCallum says the company spoke with several officers to research different experiences before they brought their scenarios to life. "They're sitting there, and all of a sudden, they're laughing, 'That happened to me last year!'"

How that relates to gang issues is that 75 TAVIS officers in two of Toronto's "priority neighbourhoods"—around Eglinton and Keele and up around Jane-Finch—get an idea of how to show they're there to help, instead of creating the impression they're soldiers of an occupying army. Having built more trust with the city's cops, Mixed Company moved on to consulting and connecting with youth, even gang members, through various social programs and organizations. And having already done plays on subjects such as homelessness, abuse and addiction, Mixed Company has learned how gang experiences can be closely related to street life.

The "press pause" technique is used in *Diss*, just as it was for the piece written for TAVIS officers. First there's a one-act "worst-case" scenario with a hip-hop DJ playing a kind of Greek chorus; in the second half of the show, the audience interacts and goes over what other paths could have been taken. "We couldn't do an hour and a half," says Malbogat.

"We'd lose our audience!" laughs McCallum.

Little by little, those watching are lured and enlisted to participate. "For us, it's easy to be sitting and coming up with options," Malbogat points out. "Because it's so easy in your head. You play it out, you win! Ego takes over, right?" He says what the show tries to do is provoke audience members to get up on their feet and publicly examine the issues involved.

Wouldn't a play like this become too didactic? Wouldn't it run the risk of talking down to its audience? "No," answers Malbogat. "I mean, that's what we're trying to take it away from. The preaching is not what we do. The whole idea is that the youth themselves are coming up and showing how they would handle the situation and make it different. So it's never coming from us as to where the solutions are."

But teenagers are, after all, hormone-filled, impulsive creatures. What if a kid says no, thinking he should blow that guy away for one of the presented scenarios?

"We're not presenting an answer, we're questioning, we're asking if it's okay," explains McCallum. "And then if they come up and say, okay, yeah, I *would* shoot that guy, we go back to the audience and say, is this reality?…Would everybody do that? And we try to challenge every single answer and see if it's the general thought and then take a look at the repercussions of things."

Interestingly enough, say Malbogat and McCallum, they saw individuals grow and evolve in attitude not only in the audience, but also within the cast taking part. McCallum likes to tell the story of Des, an Afro-Caribbean youth who "was very hungry to perform" and who was ready with dramatic options when things got slow in the audience or people were a little too scared to come up and participate. Initially, the young man's answer to a gun in a scenario was to just get another gun, show 'em who's boss. The next time around, Des offered a strategy to insult his opponent.

"And at the end of the run when he had another chance to come up," says McCallum, "he began to say, like, 'Hey, man, you don't *need* that gun, you don't need that gun. Let me see the gun for a moment, let me see the gun.' He throws the gun away. 'Dude, just, like, talk to me, I'm your bro. We don't need this shit. I know you're really angry, etcetera, etcetera.' And trying to actually talk to him, to have an effect. So it was very interesting to see Des at the start say you know, you need another gun to be powerful, then at the end of the process him being like, why don't we just talk about it, let's actually have a conversation."

Diss was never intended to be the kind of show you buy tickets for at the Edmonton Fringe Festival or you go see because you can't afford the *Showboat* revival this year. It's meant to challenge you, engage you, which is what theatre should do—otherwise you might as well hit the Cineplex Odeon or turn on the tube. The big question is: Does it create social change? How much can a carefully crafted theatre piece, even a well done one, make a difference when it hits nine city high schools?

Malbogat admits the "question looms large over everything that you do in terms of going into a school, if you're doing an anti-bully show, an anti-homophobia show, all of those. The thing is, *we know* we make a difference because of the options, because of the discussions that are provoked."

Malbogat and McCallum point to differences made in the lives of those who took part in the various shows over the years, not just *Diss*. There's Nnika, who came up from the States because her cousin is in a gang, and his enemies shot at her to get to him. She "started to blossom," says Malbogat, in training with one of the theatre professionals. She wants to continue, though as this book goes to press, survival is probably a bigger concern; she's been "couch surfing" after missing a curfew and therefore losing her spot in a shelter. There is the young man, Des, already mentioned, but who was recently having trouble with his immigration status. And there's Camille, whose young brother was killed, shot seven times in the back, after he allegedly disrespected a gang member. Malbogat says she's applied for a grant to train with the theatre company.

We don't learn what happens to Sammy after he storms out of the house at the end of the play. Malbogat and McCallum, fortunately, have some idea what has happened to a few of those whom *Diss* has touched.

Chapter Ten

Rolling Boils and Slow Simmers

L ate in the summer of 2009, Montréal police reported their city's street gang activity was down. The force's Deputy Chief Jacques Robinette conceded that, yes, a series of 20 attempted murders in the West End could be chalked up to gang violence, but having gone over the stats, he didn't think it was on the rise in the western part of the Island of Montréal. Minor crimes like simple assault and petty theft had shot up, adding to a 12 percent increase calculated so far that year for the city's overall crime rate. But crimes of extreme violence were dropping, said Robinette, who suggested that could also be said for street-gang violence.

Still, the force's West Operations Centre, based in St. Laurent, decided to place "more patrol officers out west, more people on the street, more surveillance and more targeted locations just to reassure people living in the west part of Montréal." That included the areas of Roxboro, Lachine and Côte-des-Neiges.

Robinette told a news conference that most of the violence in such neighbourhoods could be attributed to emerging street gangs, the kind his force is struggling to prevent through youth alternatives programs.

Only weeks later, however, the lull seemed to be over. Peter Lambrinakos, the chief of criminal investigations for the western region in Montréal, told a local community news website that with violent incidents on the rise in the last couple of months on the western tip of the island, police had decided to form a special investigations unit to crack down on gang activities. As the autumn began and the new unit searched 10 houses and three vehicles, officers uncovered three machine guns, a sawed-off shotgun, four knives, one ammunition belt loaded with 20 clips, a machete, around 440 different calibre bullets, three bulletproof vests, quantities of drugs and about $100,000 in cash. The cops made 25 arrests that they hoped to link to gang-related shootings.

"For sure, it was a little rivalry or a gang-drug-turf rivalry, which we ended," said Lambrinakos.

～

The mayor of Pierrefonds-Roxboro, Monique Worth, suggested that local residents might be able to sleep better.

For now, it seems that Montréal is going through a cycle of rolling boils and slow simmers when it comes to gangs. In terms of statistics, it doesn't sound like it has many. Robinette estimates there are only 25 to 30 major gangs, and only 300 to 500 hardcore members in all, not including associates. But the deputy chief says Montréal gets everything: Haitian gangs, Jamaican gangs, Asian gangs. There are even Russian gangs, who are into the usual staples of drug and gun trafficking and prostitution, but who have a sophistication that's approaching the level of the Hells Angels and the Mafia. Since the Russian mob is known to be particularly vicious, it was worth asking Robinette if they use such tactics in his city. So far, the Russians haven't been overly nasty. "We don't have those types of vicious crimes in Montréal."

The most pervasive gangs are the Crips and the Bloods, which the police refuse to name to the media to rob the gangs of free publicity. Instead, they call them the "Red" and the "Blue"—but everyone knows who they're talking about. Red for Bloods, Blue for Crips. As in Toronto and elsewhere, the gangs have no association with the original Crips and Bloods from Los Angeles. "Absolutely not," says Robinette emphatically. "Maybe some of the people know some of the people in the United States, but there's no link." Just as in Toronto, the local gangs have adopted the names for the sake of marketing fear and a reputation.

In terms of the gang food chain, however, the Crips and the Bloods in Montréal aren't much higher than their competitors. "I would say the street gangs are usually used by the biker gangs or the Mafia as the low worker on the street, to commit crimes, to sell drugs on the street, trap girls and everything," explains Robinette. "So they use those guys on the street at the very low level." (The Hells Angels and the other biker gangs will be explored in a later chapter.)

Robinette says street gangs have actually been a priority of the Montréal police for four years. In 2007, they responded at last to a public outcry over how the gangs had set up shop in the city's subway system. Back in 2005, there were 700 crimes, such as assault, in the transit network, with about 1500 property crimes, such as leaving graffiti. But the old subway security officers couldn't arrest anyone, let alone carry guns. Sixty-seven of them were absorbed into a new 132-officer unit to police the system. Robinette says that in June 2009, the unit made a major crackdown on the drug dealers in the downtown stations and made about 40 arrests.

These days, however, residents of Montréal are still more concerned with how their cops do their job on the streets, rather than under them. Things get complicated, indeed, when it comes to policing the poorer, multicultural parts of Montréal. In 2007, for instance, old frictions between the police and black communities went from slow simmer to a rolling boil once more, as an Intercultural Commission in Côte-des-Neiges accused the cops of targeting blacks as they went after gangs. A restaurant owner claimed as many as a dozen officers at a time would zero in on black youths on Victoria Avenue and demand they pony up ID and submit to searches, and young Afro-Caribbean men who were just sitting and leaning on public benches ran the risk of getting tickets for loitering.

Nor is the enmity between the police and the black population confined to one neighbourhood. Things heated up after the police force's "Advance" anti-gang strategy netted more than 1300 arrests, and its 66-member special squad for the later Projet Éclipse in 2008 cracked down on street gang members. The old accusations resurfaced, ones familiar to forces in a couple of other Canadian cities, that officers who retreat to the suburbs after their shifts are policing areas where they don't know the people or the cultural dynamics.

This is how the *Toronto Star*'s Sean Gordon described the situation in the north end of Montréal in 2008: "In an area largely dominated by the Bloods—teenaged gang-bangers and wannabes sport red kerchiefs to identify their allegiance—the cops are often seen as just another rival gang, who happen to wear the blue of their hated Crips rivals. And for the police, the gangs are holding the neighbourhood hostage and demonstrating ever more hubris, shooting at police vehicles and following cops home."

Riots broke out there in August 2008, when police shot and killed a Montréal teenager, Fredy Villanueva, after an altercation in a park. The altercation started after two officers went into the park and rousted Villanueva's older brother, a convicted robber and acquaintance of Blood gang members. In the wake of the riots, the *Star*'s Gordon argued that the reality of Montréal's cops and racial politics is "more nuanced" than a case of profiling versus rampant gangsters.

Robinette knows of this article and replies, "But the thing you need to know is that the Montréal Police Department, I would say, for the last two, three years, we're having a training plan concerning racial profiles. And I think we're the only one police department in all of Canada to have that training plan. So every police officer has to go through that training just to make them better in their activities." With about 4700 officers on the force, the program has taken "a long way to train all the officers."

What about the officers who might inadvertently touch off racial tensions just by repeatedly bugging the same kid on the street for his ID and details? The kind of scenario that Toronto's Mixed Company Theatre used in order to educate TAVIS officers there? What do officers do when young men can dress like gangstas yet are not gangsters at all?

"You need to know their name," says Robinette. "So you go after them and ask their name, and they yell at a police officer that it's racial profiling, but when you see a guy dressed like this, jewels like that, or a car like this, or girls like that, the first thing you need to know is they're probably gang-related members....But you need to investigate these guys not because they're dressed like this, not because of their colour of their skin, not because he has that type of car—you go after him *if he did something wrong.*"

A criminologist who has acted as a consultant for the force, Jean Paul Brodeur of the Université de Montréal, told the *Toronto Star* that the Montréal police suffered a sort of "reform fatigue" and that it had inevitably created confusion by trying to conduct a "reassurance policing" approach with the hard-line crackdown tactics that former New York mayor Rudy Giuliani wanted for the Big Apple. The natural result would be a lack of public confidence in the police.

Robinette argues his force hasn't been schizophrenic but is relying on an integrated approach, one of enforcement, yes, but also prevention, communication and research. "That integrated approach shows the best way to work on the street if you deal with the youth between 12 to, I would say, 16. It depends on if you deal with 16 to 20, and it depends on if you deal with the major gang members, which are probably over 20 years of age."

He advocates getting into the schools when the kids are young to present them with alternatives to crime. He says officers are "very involved" with young people in terms of football, boxing and other sports to show them other options.

And as far as the people seeing officers as just another gang in Montréal-Nord? "We're there because we need to be there, as in every part of Montréal, that's for sure."

∼

Turf does not always have to be about drugs. Take what was happening in the autumn of 2009 on a basketball court on Victoria Avenue in Montréal's Côte-des-Neiges.

For 20 years, the story goes, Filipino youths hung out on the basketball court at Coronation Elementary School, which apparently isn't that great, but served their purposes. As time went on, they couldn't presume ownership anymore, because South Asians also needed a spot to shoot hoops in what was becoming a busy few blocks. Things got ugly. Five Filipino youths were allegedly attacked on the court, with one getting a deep gash to his head and ending up in hospital for three days, while smaller fights broke out at a nearby park, a mall and on the street.

Were gangs involved? Was it a gang issue? Well, no, says Neil Castro, the secretary general of a Filipino youth support group, Kabataang Montréal. What it's really about is economic marginalization and a lack of support and services for the Filipino community, the fastest growing ethnic population in Côte-des-Neiges. Yes, there were Filipino gangs in the neighbourhood once upon a time, but that's old news. And Kabataang Montréal has seen it all before.

In fact, one of the organization's founders, Roderick Carreon, told the *Montréal Mirror* in 2003 that he got involved in gangs soon after he arrived in Canada and "went through the same crap, made the same mistakes," but later got a taste of politics after being fired from a factory job. "All the so-called gangs were formed in schools as a kind of self-defence mechanism against racism, being isolated and taken from one place to another."

Back in 2000, when Kabataang Montréal was formed, says Neil Castro, one of the issues they actually first dealt with was youth violence—only at that time it was young Filipinos fighting among themselves. "A lot of people like to label them gangs, but really, from our knowledge, it wasn't gangs, it was just a bunch of youth who were coming together to look for that kind of security, that belonging. A lot of them have been alienated at school, a lot of them were newly arrived immigrants struggling to learn French, having many, many different barriers and difficulties while they were at school, so they banded together for protection, for belonging."

The violence broke out, says Castro, over petty issues—looking at someone's girlfriend wrong, that sort of thing. "Instead of them realizing that they had a lot of com-monalities, a lot of similarities, they would take it out on each other...instead of taking the time to really look at how they're going through the same thing together."

But as these young people got older (like Roderick Carreon), they faced the reality that they needed jobs and had to work. They took on family responsibilities; they grew up and began to examine the causes of their community's problems. They "aged out," as some gang members do, and they became involved in their community; they joined organizations and started sports programs. Castro, who is in his 30s, says, "Even since I've been involved since 2004, I've seen two different waves of youth pass through our organization. So on the streets and basketball courts, I've seen two different sets already."

But the organization sees the same challenges facing the next wave of young people: low wages, poor working conditions, systemic racism, high dropout rates from high school and a lack of resources and infrastructure. "There's a clear link between marginalized youth members living in a ghettoized, populated area and youth violence," says Carreon. "This speaks to a lack of support for the youth."

Having witnessed the cycle before, the group quickly moved to address the latest sporadic outbursts of violence. Castro told a news conference that going after the individuals involved wouldn't end the problem. Instead, says Castro, the community needs to look at the reasons why youth feel they have to form groups to protect themselves. Originally, Kabataang Montréal wanted to hold the news conference with an organization representing the South Asian community, but it couldn't find one to participate in time.

He's frustrated that the two ethnic groups have had such difficulty linking up to address issues they both face. "I mean, we live together, we see each other on the streets

every day, but when it comes to organizing, our organizations can't find each other. It really goes to show that kind
of divisiveness even within different immigrant groups.…
Now we got politicians coming out and trying to introduce
us to each other, play the matchmaker, but really, why did it
have to come to this point? Why is it now that they're moving? So we're looking at all these factors on why we're the
way we are today."

He told the *Montréal Gazette* he wanted police to be
aware of the situation, but at the same time, he was concerned that officers would stop every single Filipino and
South Asian person they saw. A police official had to admit
she didn't know anything about the tension between Filipino and South Asian youth until the day before the *Gazette*
approached her for an interview.

"When crimes go unreported, it's hard to find solutions and work together on this," Commander Simonetta
Barth told the newspaper.

The point can be made that the police can't be
expected to react to a crime until they're told about it, but
Castro replies, "For us, we're not working for the police,
I mean, we're serving our youth." He says the organization
did encourage victims of violence to step forward and file
a report, but in the end, if they chose not to, these young
people can't be forced to do it.

And Castro says young people in his community have
long put up with racial profiling and police harassment.

In addition to the usual stops and demands for ID, he says it can also take subtle forms, such as an officer bugging a young person on a basketball court over what they're wearing or the logo on a T-shirt. "All these subtle little harassments that the youth have to live with every day."

He says the Filipino community has tried to make its concerns known to the police, but the profiling goes on. "They come out to the public and say they're doing things, but the reality is what we're experiencing on the street."

That brings us back to the same question of trust as posed in the chapter on Toronto. If an ethnic or immigrant community doesn't trust the police, it stands to lose because it needs policing just like any other community, so couldn't gangs take advantage of a climate of suspicion and paranoia?

"The police are meant to serve and protect," replies Castro. "The question is: serve and protect whom? There is a large mistrust between our youth and the police, but this is also shared with our wider community because we do not feel that the police are there for us. If any change in the relationship between cops and communities of colour is to happen, it must come from them because they are the perpetrators of racial profiling, harassment, brutality and oppression. And they have guns."

In discussing the lack of trust between the police and the ethnic communities, Deputy Chief Robinette says, "We need to work with the population, we need to take the population as a partner with the police officers." But Neil Castro is unconvinced. He says things haven't changed. The two sides seem to be at an impasse.

And so for now, the gang the Filipinos in Côte-des-Neiges may fear most is the one the *Star* suggested that many fear in Montréal's north end—the boys in blue.

Chapter Eleven

The Self-Cleaning Oven

Halifax had a rough year in 2008 when it came to gangs. While Calgary was still wondering what was behind the bad blood between FOB and the FK Killers, and Toronto's York South-Weston was soon to heat up with the rivalry between the Five Point Generalz and the Gatorz, the beautiful port city of Nova Scotia had a gang war all its own. On first impression, it sounds like a feud between two of the most notorious criminal families in the city, ones that have roots—and records—going back 20 years. As the *Halifax Chronicle Herald* put it, "Back in the day, some of these players made money and a name for themselves— together." Then you find out it's not even that simple.

The patriarchs of both families have done hard federal time. Terry Marriott Sr. has racked up more than

32 years over drugs and other offences. In 1988, he was charged with murder after what's believed to have been a drug-related shooting left one man dead on a Halifax street. Marriott walked away in 1991 with an acquittal.

That was probably the high point for him in the '90s. In 1998, Marriott's brother Ricky, already facing drug charges, was shot in his own house and died, while his girlfriend died in hospital from her injuries four days later. In 2000, Marriott's other brother, Billy—facing trial for the murder of a Hells Angels associate—hanged himself in a jail cell. Another trial heard testimony that Marriott believed his brother Billy had murdered Ricky, though the rest of the family may not hold that view.

As the millennium came to a close, drug dealing became a father-and-son business. In 1999, a joint-forces investigation going after street dealers scooped up both Marriott Sr. and his son, Terry Jr., among 40 charged suspects. Dad got four years for trafficking while the chip off the ol' block got four and a half for possession. Nor would that be the last that the federal penitentiary system saw of Terry Jr. The National Parole Board even told the son at one point to stay away from his father because of his criminal history.

Then there is the Melvin family. In 1991, police stopped a truck on the highway near Chester and seized more than three and a half tonnes of hashish they believed had come in from a Panamanian ship. Among the 10 suspects charged was Jimmy Melvin Sr., who would get eight years, but would not learn to stay away from drugs on ships. His next caper sounds like something out of Halifax's heritage of pirates and privateers.

In late 1992, the U.S. Coast Guard spent 19 hours pursuing a Spanish vessel carrying about three tonnes of cocaine through choppy seas, only to have the ship sink the next day off the coast of Newfoundland. But Jimmy Melvin didn't know that, and he wasted a couple of days with an associate—who then became a witness for the Crown— trying to find the ship so he could unload the drugs for the Hells Angels. He was sentenced to five and half years in 1997 for conspiracy to traffic cocaine. In 2001, he was sentenced to another six years and three months for selling hashish.

By the summer of the next year, the Marriott and Melvin names could be lumped together in court documents. An undercover police probe, Operation Midway, dragged 81 suspects into its net, including associates of both families. A drug dealer turned police informant—who ran a "crack shop" in Herring Cove Road—testified how the younger generation of Melvins and Marriotts were behind a drug ring in the city: Terry Marriott Sr.'s son, Brian James Bremner (known as B.J. Marriott), a cousin, Gary "Boo" Boudreau, and Jimmy Melvin Jr.

Boudreau got more than six years for drug and weapons offences. Although he managed to stay out of jail after getting out, there was still trouble coming his way—

his tanning salon in Herring Cove Road was firebombed in 2006. B.J. Marriott was eventually convicted of drug smuggling and trafficking charges and is now in a Prairie prison facility for manslaughter, assault and weapons convictions; he has a parole board hearing in 2011. The family tree of convictions doesn't stop there—his mother and uncle received conditional sentences. Jimmy Melvin Jr.'s mother and his girlfriend also received sentences at the same time. Interestingly, neither of the family patriarchs were picked up during this investigation.

For Melvin Jr., it must have turned into a case of lawyer's papers being passed between bars. He was already in jail when Operation Midway started collaring suspects, and he was later sentenced to three years for trying to get drugs smuggled to him in prison through the drug ring. "That was to be served on top of a two-year term he received in December 2002 for possessing cocaine for the purpose of trafficking in May 2001," reported the *Chronicle Herald*, doing its best to relay all the confusing details. "His sentence ended on May 17, 2006, but he had been in custody in relation to other charges until he was ordered released" in November 2008. The Crown had to withdraw its charges against him over a home invasion, saying there was no chance of a conviction since witnesses had changed their stories.

Somewhere along the line, things apparently turned ugly between members of the two families, though only the insiders know the original cause.

"At one point in the past, for some reason, somebody decided they wanted to branch out on their own or franchise, if you will, and it's kind of sped off from there," reasons Superintendent Don Spicer of the Halifax Regional Police. "It's not like there's a large family of the Melvins and a large family of the Marriotts, you know, the Hatfields and the McCoys. It's one or two people in each family who then have friends or hangers-on who look up to them for one reason or another who are hanging with them....I think if there was a spinoff at all, it would have been the Melvins spinning off."

However the split happened, in late 2002, someone tossed a Molotov cocktail and fired five shots at a house owned by Melvin Sr. The suburban community of Spryfield turned into ground zero for a string of fire bombings and shootings at various homes and businesses.

But here's the kicker—it's not a clear-cut case of one family versus the other. There are Marriotts who work with Melvins, and Melvin relatives who will do business with Marriotts. The word is that Terry Marriott Jr., before he was shot to death in a Harrietsfield bungalow in the winter of 2009, was working with Melvins.

"They say the most confusing day in Spryfield is Father's Day," says reporter Rob Gordon, who has covered a lot of the gang action for the CBC in Nova Scotia. "Parts of it, particularly the parts they live in and stuff, are just wild. I mean it's like no other rules in any other place. Half of them are related, the other half aren't, some of them might be related and not know it, others might be related but not telling anybody, I mean, it's all over the place."

Sometimes the family members need a scorecard themselves for who they're talking to. Gordon says that years ago, he stopped into a bar owned by Melvin Sr. to have a drink with a friend who worked there as a short-order cook. Melvin Sr. wound up at the table. For Gordon, it was supposed to be a couple of beers with his friend, not an attempt to get a story. Not long after, he went to court to cover a drug case and saw Melvin Sr. sitting in the public gallery. He was surprised to see the journalist there and later walked up, demanding, "Are you heat?"

"No, no, I'm a reporter," explained Gordon.

"Aw, fuck, good, 'cause I can usually tell the heat. Didn't think you were."

~

Until recently, it looked as if the fight would stay between the families. What did it matter if those who were shot or killed weren't innocents? Halifax cops apparently call the situation the "self-cleaning oven." That changed in 2008—and the oven heat that set off the fire alarms was felt right downtown, right in front of a children's hospital.

Much of the escalation in violence was blamed on the release late that year of Jimmy Melvin Jr. Days after he was freed, someone shot at his father and an associate outside a pizza place in Spryfield; both were unhurt. The next day one of the Melvin associates was wounded when multiple shots were fired right in front of the IWK Health Centre. The following month, Melvin Jr. took two bullets in his upper body outside an apartment block. Police didn't see the shooting, even though they were actually conducting surveillance on him at the time. Then Marriott Jr. was killed, and in April, Melvin Jr. was a target again. This time, gunshot wounds resulted in him having to use a colostomy bag. The violence didn't stop. Weeks after that, gunfire hit his father's house.

As all this went on, the charges against Melvin Jr. continued to pile up. As the chronicle of the feud was being drafted for *Gangs in Canada*, Halifax Regional Police stopped a vehicle in which Melvin Jr. was riding in Dartmouth on a September night. They arrested him over a prohibited weapon—a "push knife," with a blade that protrudes between the fingers—as well as drugs and drug paraphernalia. He was still awaiting trial over death threats to a police officer and arson and mischief charges over a fire in a prison cell.

But Melvin Jr. appears to enjoy the attention. For a court appearance over the death threats, he made squealing noises when he was brought into provincial court. The night his father was shot at outside the pizza joint, Melvin's behaviour was particularly memorable for reporters. Rob Gordon says that while Spryfield kids as young as 10 or 12 looked on, a car with Melvin Jr. as the passenger pulled up onto the sidewalk near the crime scene. Melvin jumped out of the car with an open beer in his hand and brushed past a female police officer.

"Hey!" she called as he lifted the yellow caution tape.

"Go fuck yourself," barked Melvin as he kept on moving.

Gordon says the officer didn't do anything, letting Melvin go into the pizza place where dozens of detectives and officers were already going about the business of investigation. After yelling and screaming at the cops, he finished his beer, came out and shouted for the TV cameras beside the caution tape, "There's no rats in the Melvin family! There's no rats in the Melvin family! [sic]" There are still clips of this floating around the Internet, with Melvin poking his head outside his associate's car as it drove away, shouting, "Death before dishonour!" Then he punctuated this confusing battle cry with a high-pitched whoop.

"Those little kids, those kids who were watching it, just saw Superman," says Gordon. "It was sad. I actually asked the police chief about it. 'Why? Why does he get to do that?'" Gordon was not impressed with what he calls the chief's "typical cop answer" that officers on the street must be left with the discretion of when to move in on a situation.

In 2009, Melvin Jr. launched his own website, real-livestreetshit.com. For many, it is a repulsive product. And he got exactly the kind of attention he wanted for its launch. With a banner suggesting you join the site on Facebook and follow it on Twitter, the recent home page offered a video set to hip-hop music made up of clips about "Jimmy Melvin on the News." You get a string of anchors mentioning his name with "Jimmy Melvin…Jimmy Melvin…Jimmy Melvin" all running together like a four-year-old's chant.

When the site was launched, the CBC in Nova Scotia led with it as its top story for the six o' clock news on a Tuesday night in May, devoting more than two and a half minutes to what it called Melvin's "bizarre scheme": a Maritime white boy finishing up his 20s by using gangsta slang and "Yo" to suggest he actually is a teenager from Compton; Melvin showing off his injuries and flashing his money while bragging, "Who wants to get rich or die? I know I ain't dying, and I'm rich." The video apparently didn't last long, as it violated certain content restrictions. No problem. The website now features CBC's own item, taken off YouTube, despite reporter Rob Gordon's tart observation that "This is all about Jimmy—Jimmy Melvin as his own hero."

Gordon strikes an apologetic note when quizzed about the news value of reporting on the website. "That was silly, you're right there. I'm an old newspaper guy, so if you make something a headline, what you're saying is that's the most important story in Nova Scotia today." And while he sees some value in pointing out to people how Melvin was celebrating himself, he certainly doesn't believe it should have been the lead. "Every time we run a Melvin story, we get letters from people: Will you guys stop turning this guy into a hero? Just stop doing that. And I got to tell you, I'm torn."

Melvin is not, even though Gordon has clearly gone after him with a critical eye. Another story lifted for the website followed his application to work outside the province. In the story, Gordon quietly demands to know from both Melvin's lawyer and the Crown prosecutor whether the convicted drug dealer has ever held a job in his life.

The love of attention isn't something his father or anyone in either of the two notorious families seems to share. Gordon says Melvin Sr. appears to be "mortified" by the public shenanigans of his son, often trying to pull him away from the cameras. According to Gordon, Marriott Sr., while not being outright rude, has nothing to say to reporters when they come charging up.

So if Jimmy Melvin Jr.'s persona is merely for the cameras, perhaps only he and his close associates know. "The way he portrays himself in the media is no different than the way he portrays himself with us," says Superintendent Spicer.

In BC, there was a fellow who made the news through his inflammatory comments and behaviour, who seemed to relish attention. His name was Bindy Johal. And we know what happened to him.

～

Despite the likes of Melvin Jr. still making headlines, Halifax itself is not yet a battlefield like Vancouver or even reaching the violence level of a Winnipeg, according to Superintendent Don Spicer. "Far from it. I would say probably as recent as two years ago, if we were doing this interview, I would have told you we had about eight gangs, and we're down to four from all the intelligence that we have…"

If that's true, it's something of a small miracle for the port city, especially when you consider it was leading the list in terms of violent cities per capita in Canada in 2004.

Here, too, cops changed tactics as they had to in Vancouver and Calgary. One simple change was to send out uniforms to pound the pavement again, instead of having them in their patrol cars doing the slow trawl through the neighbourhoods. "Somebody from one of the communities coined the phrase a couple of years ago, they called them 'the police officers with no feet,'" says Spicer. "You see them from the shoulder up as they're driving by." So, more officers on foot. Then the force launched Operation Breach.

While many young people were being picked up for crimes and then released on conditions, there wasn't any enforcement in place to make sure those conditions were met. The cops targeted the most likely prolific offenders and went down their checklists again and again to make sure the offenders were complying—if not, back they went. "We've been doing this since 2005, and our crime rate has been dropping every year since." The force has also organized quick response units to deal in part with gangs, with divisional commanders able to quickly deploy teams of officers available in either plain clothes or uniform detail.

"On the other end of the scale—I know it's not something necessarily when you're talking about gangs, it's not the glorious stuff," says Spicer, but some officers are also involved in homework clubs for students and reading and literacy clubs.

Rob Gordon, the newspaperman-turned-broadcaster, the professional observer, is not so sure things are improving. While he grants that police likely have got a lot of control over the situation, and while, knock wood, so far there have been few, if any, innocents seriously hurt in the gang war, public perception in Halifax is quite different. He would expect most people to say the gang problem has gotten worse. "I think if you asked anybody on the street here, were the police winning the battles against the gangs? And they would go, 'Hell, no.'"

As even the police concede, the city still sees its share of gunplay and shootings. Sometimes the duration of the violence may even have more to do with incompetence than with ruthless determination. Given that Melvin Jr., for instance, has been shot more than once and multiple attempts have been made on Melvin Sr., Gordon was prompted to ask police how many times it takes to shoot someone before you actually get it right and hit him?

The answer from veteran cops tells a lot about our gangsters, and according to them, this has even become a topic of conversation in police and pathology circles. After all, the victims can be shot three or four times, and while bleeding, are still able to flee until they're hunted down and shot in the head. The crime scenes can be Jackson Pollack blood canvases.

"They said it's because they watch gangster rap videos and they're holding the gun the wrong way," says Gordon. "Instead of holding it up and down and pointing it at the belly like the old guys, the old gangsters would do—you point it at your belt buckle, pull the trigger, the gun pulls up a bit and you hit 'em square in the chest, right? What these guys do is they hold the gun sideways like in the rap videos, so when you pull the trigger it pulls the gun from the left to the right. So that even if you're really close to somebody, if you're aiming at their chest, and you pull the trigger, the gun pulls out to the right." And hits an arm or misses the target altogether.

Lately, the "self-cleaning oven" has shown some very messy streaks and smears.

Chapter Twelve

Patchwork: How the Hells Angels Rule

Perhaps the thing that would surprise most Canadians about the Hells Angels (HA) is just how much of a Canadian institution they truly are. In fact, there are more club members *here* per capita than in any other country—including the United States. Think about that for a moment—*there are more Hells Angels in Canada than anywhere else.*

And one of the reasons why they're here, which pretty much no one contests, is Canada's own fault.

They are also at the top of the heap, so much so that Len Isnor doesn't even think of them in the same way as the other gangs discussed so far in this book. To him, they're different animals. "Gangs are *unorganized* crime," he says flatly. "I mean, you might think that they're organized enough, but they don't have the hierarchy, they don't have the structure, they don't have the colours, they don't have the network across the country...."

Isnor ought to know. With his stout cop's build and right-angle cop haircut, it's easy to pick him out of a crowd and believe he is a detective sergeant with the Ontario Provincial Police. You believe he's head of the multi-force, OPP-led Biker Enforcement Unit because his knowledge of biker gangs, especially the Hells Angels, is positively encyclopaedic. For him, there is no comparison.

Other gangs, he points out, are very hands on, doing the dirty work and violence themselves. "They're not getting rich. The odd guy is, but he's also closer to the grave or going to jail than being a millionaire. I mean, our jails are full of gang members." By comparison, the Hells Angels are smart enough to regularly keep at arm's length, using other gangs to distribute drugs, launder money and perform other criminal activities. It's the difference between the amateur leagues and the pros. The Zig Zag Crew of Manitoba, for instance, has been a major "farm team" for the HA.

It's been an uphill battle for law enforcement, thanks in part to the gang's powerful structure and system, which puts them on a level that traditional organized crime enjoyed back in the 1940s and '50s.

"Think about it," says Isnor. "You, tomorrow, can be a gang member." Not so, as far as the Hells Angels are concerned. You pay your dues over *years*.

The process is this. First, someone within the club must know you for at least five years. You're brought to the clubhouse and introduced around, and your sponsor swears up and down that you have never been a cop and will never screw over your new pals. So you become a "friend," and after one year, you must pass a unanimous vote to decide whether or not you'll be allowed to be a "hang-around member." You get a little patch on your vest that might say "Toronto"—but that's all it says. There's no other insignia, and you've still got a long way to go. At the end of another year as a hang-around, you need *another* unanimous vote from club members to be a "prospect." You now get a patch that has "Prospect" above "Toronto," and you get "MC" (as in "Motorcycle Club") on your jacket. It will be another year and yet another vote before you've earned your full colours and become a "full-patch member" entitled to wear the famous winged death's-head.

"Now, if I'm an undercover cop, and I want to infiltrate the Hells Angels," says Isnor, "I got to start tomorrow, I got to find a Hells Angels member to know me for five years...." It's an eight-year process that works quite brilliantly to keep cops out.

All the while, recruits are being watched and assessed. As they move up the ranks, trust is slowly built. A hang-around isn't allowed to be in the clubhouse alone, a privilege that only starts when you become a prospect. You might be asked to prove yourself, and if club members smell a cop or something else they don't like, they may ask you to commit a criminal offence.

The club's system, however, is not foolproof. In BC, a doorman at a strip club in downtown Vancouver became a police informant in 2003, earning $2000 a month by feeding the cops intelligence. In 2004, he signed a contract with the cops that gave him the opportunity to earn up to $1 million.

Money was also the motivation for Steven Gault, a full-patch member, to turn informant. As part of a multi-force, 18-month investigation dubbed "Project Tandem," he earned almost $1 million by feeding police information and wearing a body pack to record the leader of the Niagara Hells Angels blabbing about the cocaine trade. In the recordings, Gerald "Skinny" Ward complained about how hard it was to find new recruits and about the problem of certain bikers getting stoned on their own supply of drugs. He got a sentence of 14 years.

Isnor, who handled Gault, readily admits, "He was paid well, but to put a price on things like this, it's a bargain for the taxpayers. I mean, for us in Project Tandem, we put away 15 Hells Angels, and that includes just prospects. And to do 15 Hells Angels on our own without somebody like that—*huge* price tag."

There are the wiretap monitors the cops would need, the surveillance teams, not to mention thousands of personnel hours combing through phone calls, figuring out target patterns for surveillance, all while trying to prove connections that will hold up in court. As far as Isnor is concerned, Gault did a great job. "We pay some agent X amount of dollars. That price tag is substantially less than what it would cost us if we did it by traditional means."

It is not just Isnor, his fellow cops and Crown prosecutors praising such methods. Even some defence lawyers have admitted that Project Tandem had the goods on their clients, to the point where their grudging surrender sounds almost comical. "I told my client to plead guilty," a defence lawyer told the *National Post*. "The writing was on the wall."

Isnor paints a disturbing picture of just how extensive the network is for an international club that keeps saying it's only a bunch of guys who enjoy riding motorcycles.

"Most people say, well, the Hells Angels don't affect me, so I don't give a shit about the Hells Angels, but they do," says Isnor. "I mean, your children are getting dope in the schools that…most likely comes from the Hells Angels. Your insurance rates are what they are because they're stealing motorcycles and cars all across this country. And they're laundering their money through businesses that file for bankruptcy where the government is basically bailing them out with your tax dollars. The Hells Angels will affect every single person on this planet."

～

The history of the Hells Angels in the United States is, of course, fairly well known. Founded in the late 1940s and early '50s in California as the "Pissed Off Bastards of Bloomington," they took the name Hells Angels from World War I and II fighter squadrons—not that any of the bikers were in such squadrons. They liked to party. They liked to make trouble. The roar of the Harley-Davidson hit a chord in the post-war angst of the 1950s and '60s so that from Marlon Brando in the 1953 film, *The Wild One*, which wasn't about the Angels per se but was close enough, to Jack Nicholson in a 1967 movie actually called *Hells Angels on Wheels*, the motorcycle club's reputation grew.

Throw in a 1966 investigative book by Hunter S. Thompson, himself a self-promoter who liked to celebrate his drunken, drug-induced excesses, as well as a knife murder by a club member at the Rolling Stones concert in Altamont in 1969, and the rep expanded from infamy to sinister legend.

The Hells Angels are now quite literally a franchise organization with territory that includes the West Coast of North America and Australia, as well as Britain and Germany. Up here in quiet, supposedly dull Canada, we already had biker gangs, like the Red Devils of Hamilton, Ontario, whose history dates back to the late 1940s. Police ignored them as small-fry irritants and troublemakers, certainly not to be considered organized crime. In their groundbreaking book on the Hells Angels in Canada, *The Road to Hell*, investigative reporters Julian Sher and William Marsden quote one inspector as flatly admitting, "No one was targeting them from an enforcement perspective."

In fact, Sher and Marsden profile an old-school Montréal police veteran, André Bouchard, who relished beating up members of a small-time biker gang, the Popeyes. At the time, the Popeyes were mostly enforcers, running prostitution rings and acting as blunt instruments for the more sophisticated Mafia and the Dubois mob. "You saw a guy walking up the street in his colours, you kicked the shit out of him, and that was it." The cops could humiliate a biker by literally ripping the club patch off his jacket.

But those were the days before constitutional rights, when the police could do almost whatever they wanted. The story of the modern biker gangs in this country, especially the Hells Angels, is a surreal, convoluted one. It sounds like part feudal warfare, part history of the Borgia family and part comic book.

The American biker club, the Outlaws, was already staking a claim in Canada in 1977. As a port city, Montréal has been key to the drug trade, and Isnor is quick to offer a reminder that it's easier to get drugs into Montréal than into New York or Baltimore. The Outlaws wanted it, and to get it, they started to absorb the gang that was the major competition for the Popeyes, Satan's Choice. Satan's Choice members would "patch over" to become Outlaw members.

The American Hells Angels saw a crucial link in the drug chain potentially being lost, so in December 1977, the winged, helmeted death's-head emblem made its first appearance in a Canadian chapter in a new operation in

Sorel, on the outskirts of Montréal. Thirty-five members of the Popeyes would patch over to the HA.

While many people have heard about the gang war between the Hells Angels and their rivals, Rock Machine, in the 1990s, the Hells Angels first had a bloody war with the Outlaws. The war lasted from 1977 to the mid-1980s, when the Outlaws were run out of Montréal, and the Hells Angels acquired a near-monopoly over the drug trade coming into the city.

The HA then decided to strategically capture the port on the other side of the country—Vancouver. By 1986, the Hells Angels were feeling so at home in BC that the Nanaimo chapter hosted a lavish party for both local and international members on a 17-acre property. Just as regular British Columbians are known for being more laid back than people in other parts of Canada, the Hells Angels there decided to do things differently than their Québec cousins.

"Québec did everything by violence. They muscled their way in, took over the market, made a lot of money," explains Isnor. In BC, "those guys did everything by diplomacy."

At the time, laws regarding criminal organizations and proceeds of crime were different and more lax, which allowed the BC Hells Angels to legitimize some of their businesses. One member even bought Safeway stores.

In Québec, however, you couldn't call the Hells Angels laid back. When Laval members started snorting too much of what they were supposed to sell in 1985, members from Lennoxville killed five of them, then wrapped the bodies in chains, weighted them with bricks and dumped them into the St. Lawrence River.

But the two men credited with really building the HA in Canada are Maurice "Mom" Boucher and Walter "Nurget" Stadnick. They were among a small band who formed a new kind of elite unit within the Hells Angels, the Nomads. They were based out of Montréal but didn't have to pay allegiance to a specific club. Mom Boucher was in charge.

Boucher was a tall, stocky, working-class Québecois and high-school dropout. By the time he joined the Hells Angels, he already had serious convictions for crimes such as armed robbery and holding a knife to a woman's throat while he sexually assaulted her. As his power grew, the spectacled, smiling Boucher boasted he had spies within law enforcement and took his fellow Hells Angels—in full colours—down to the café below the headquarters of the Montréal police's homicide and anti-gang squad where police liked to have their morning coffee. It infuriated the old-school cops like André Bouchard, who is quoted in *The Road to Hell* as saying that 20 years earlier, "we would have thumped the son of a bitch. Because you do not intimidate a cop. You've got to show them, 'I'm not afraid of you, you prick.'"

The word "ruthless" barely covers Mom Boucher. As it became clear in the late 1990s that authorities had an informant within the club, he decided that a demonstration was in order to scare bikers into never testifying or turning snitch. With a logic that only Boucher could understand, he decided to do this by planning the murders of prison guards, cops, prosecutors and even judges. He was tried—and at first acquitted—of the murders of two correctional officers. Ironically, what helped sink him was the very thing he wanted to prevent with his wave of murders—one of his own turned informant, Stephane "Godasse" Gagné, the man who carried out the killings.

Walter "Nurget" Stadnick (how he got the nickname has never been quite clear) was a peculiar figure among the mostly Francophone Angels—a short, middleweight Anglo from Hamilton. Stadnick had managed to avoid flying bullets and bombs in biker feuds even before he patched over to the Hells—only to be almost killed when a priest drove through a stop sign because he was desperate to see Pope John Paul II on his first trip to Canada. In the collision, the gas tank on Stadnick's bike exploded, and he was badly burned. Then during the 1980s, some members of the Outlaws wanted to fire   a rocket launcher at the Rebel Roadhouse, the watering hole in Hamilton that Stadnick managed in all but name and where he kept an office. A timely arrest prevented the rocket from being shot into the bar.

Stadnick reportedly became national president of the Hells Angels in Canada in 1988 by default. He was the most senior one left after many other members had gone to jail or were killed. And it certainly was good to be king. When he wasn't riding his hog or one of his other motorcycles, the president drove around in a Jaguar. His home boasted a black marble countertop in the kitchen and a bathroom with a Jacuzzi and a built-in television. His master bedroom was decorated in the Hells Angels colours of red and white.

What Stadnick brought to the HA table, what made him unique, was his dream of empire. He imagined a coast-to-coast franchise for the HA, and as Sher and Marsden chronicle in *The Road to Hell*, he was constantly working to expand the reach of the club into other parts of the country, such as Winnipeg and especially Ontario, a prized market for the drug trade with its higher population. The approach to capture Ontario during the 1990s, according to Detective-Sergeant Len Isnor, was very much like the one applied in BC, one of diplomacy.

The fiercest competition for the Hells Angels was back in their Canadian base of Québec. Many smaller criminal gangs, mob families and other groups banded together to form "The Dark Circle" (and, yes, they really called it that). Included in the Circle was Rock Machine, a rival biker gang founded by Salvatore Cazzetta and his brother, Giovanni, who had once been friends of Mom Boucher in his earliest biker club.

"The newspapers report it as a Rock Machine–Hells Angels war," says Isnor, "but really, it's a Dark Circle war, because Rock Machine are the big ones, and they're not really a motorcycle gang at first, but they evolve into a motorcycle gang as the 1990s go through, because everybody's saying, 'Who are these Rock Machine guys? They're doing pretty good...'"

The subsequent biker war claimed more than 160 lives in Québec, with shootings and bombings, including the death of an 11-year-old boy who was killed when a piece of shrapnel from an exploding Jeep sliced into his brain. But often the efforts of the Montréal police, the SQ and the RCMP to get the Angels off the street were hampered by mistrust, in-fighting, episodes of corruption, unusual tactics and, arguably, some astonishing incompetence.

A bisexual, boyish-looking biker in wire-rimmed glasses, Dany Kane, approached the Mounties in 1994 to become an informant. Two years later, to give Kane a financial front to avoid suspicion from his biker pals and ostensibly to keep him out of trouble, the RCMP paid him more than $30,000 to set up a short-lived sex magazine. Kane even managed to drive to Halifax without his Mountie handlers' knowledge to commit a contract killing. He walked free because of a declared mistrial and went back to being an informant. Apparently tortured by self-doubt, he committed suicide in his garage in 2000.

Meanwhile, the Bandidos biker gang, originally from Texas, was watching the success of Rock Machine and liked what it saw as the Hell Angel's competitor opened clubs in Toronto, Kingston and London. Rock Machine, says Len

Isnor, changed their colours to the reverse of the Bandidos, which are red and gold; a symbolic act that usually shows the affiliation of a puppet club to a bigger one. Ontario underwent a dizzying series of shifting allegiances as the HA moved to keep up, taking in clubs such as Satan's Choice and the Para-Dice Riders.

Back in Québec that same year of 2000, high-profile crime reporter Michel Auger was shot in the back in the parking lot of his workplace, *Journal de Montréal.* Amazingly, he survived. But the people of Québec had by now gotten their fill of violence and started marching in protests by the thousands. With even the Mafia worried over a possible crackdown to appease public outrage, the HA and Rock Machine made a great show of a biker summit and truce. Yet the bombs and the slaughter of complete innocents went on, and it galvanized communities, putting more pressure on the cops.

In a moment of triumph, the Montréal police and the Sûreté du Québec still squabbled over who got to arrest Mom Boucher after the Québec Court of Appeal ordered a new trial for the prison guard murders. When he was convicted in 2002, Boucher got a life sentence with no chance of parole for 25 years. He has been kept in a super-maximum-security penitentiary in Ste. Anne des Plaines, north of Montréal. Although he's housed in the block where other Hells Angels are kept, there have still been attempts on his life.

About three months before Boucher's conviction, 400 Hells Angels from across the country descended on Toronto for a convention. Mayor Mel Lastman gushed, "You know, they are just a nice bunch of guys." The disgusted mother of the little boy in Québec killed by bomb shrapnel wanted the mayor to resign. Lastman has never been a stranger to controversy; a reporter once claimed the flamboyant mayor barked death threats at him for investigating his daughter's shoplifting, and he caused international headlines—and embarrassment for Toronto—with jokes about cannibals before a trip to Kenya. When challenged over the "nice bunch of guys" he was hanging out with, Lastman insisted he didn't know the Hells Angels were involved with drug trafficking.

Despite the Toronto mayor's ignorance, police forces across the country knew exactly who they were dealing with and poured on the heat. In the massive Operation Springtime in 2001, more than 2000 officers from different forces went after the HA in Québec, particularly the Nomads; in Operation Hammer later that same year, the Hells Angels clubhouse was seized in Halifax. But the icing on the cake must have been when Walter Stadnick was arrested while on holiday in Montego Bay by a Jamaican SWAT team and brought back to Canada. Given the harshness of Jamaican prisons, one of the Mounties transporting Stadnick home to Canada sarcastically offered to arrange a prolonged stay in Kingston for the top-ranking biker.

But Stadnick was reportedly cocky. "Couple more weeks—I'd be running this place!"

He also told his police chaperons on the flight home that he didn't think there was any evidence against him and that he would likely spend a year in prison, at most. Facing 23 counts of murder, conspiracy to commit murder, drug trafficking and gangsterism, Stadnick chose to take his chances with a trial before a judge instead of a jury. He managed to beat the rap on the first-degree murder charges.

"It is true that Stadnick was active in arranging for biker clubs outside of...Québec to become associated with the Hells Angels for the purpose of trafficking drugs," said Superior Court Judge Jerry Zigman when he reached his verdict in 2004. "However, there was no evidence led before the court to indicate that those who opposed him were murdered or harmed in any way."

But while the judge didn't hear any evidence that Stadnick had shot anyone or ordered executions, he still sentenced him to 20 years on the other charges, the most important for the prosecution being his participation in a criminal organization. The court had heard how confidential police files—stolen from an OPP computer—were found in police raids on Stadnick's home and the Ancaster home of Daniel "Pup" Stockford, the vice-president of the Québec Nomads and a professional movie stuntman. The Hells Angels had used the files and accompanying photos to hunt down and murder their gang rivals.

"The reason why Stockford had the binder of photos at his residence was because he was a participant in the conspiracy to murder them," the judge noted tartly. "He certainly did not have the pictures at his residence so that he could admire the faces of his enemies."

Stadnick and Stockford lost appeals of their convictions in 2009.

The war between law enforcement and the Hells Angels, however, goes on. In addition to the success of the more recent Project Tandem, Operation SharQc (Stratégie Hells Angels Région Québec) in the spring of 2009 "vacuumed up the province's remaining Angels" as William Marsden put it for the *Montréal Gazette*. As well as drug trafficking, they faced charges that went all the way back to the biker war with Rock Machine, the Bandidos and the Dark Circle.

It's a huge case for prosecutors, but as Marsden pointed out, "defence lawyers could have a field day tying the court procedures in knots."

∾

When it comes to the lay of the land today in Ontario and Québec, Len Isnor says, "Right now, we have basically an open market, and that's why your gangs are starting to really take off, because we have 50 of the 185 Hells Angels in jail right now here in Ontario. One hundred and twelve of the 114 Hells Angels in Québec are in jail....We've got

the bikers against the wall, and it's creating a great environment for these gangs to move in and take things over."

That doesn't mean the Hells Angels are out of the
game, not by a long shot. Even as this book was being prepared, the CBC's French language service reported that
a Hells Angels member from the Sherbrooke chapter allegedly had a hand in manipulating labour politics. The CBC
claims he helped persuade a candidate to drop out of an
internal election to head one of the biggest construction
unions in Québec.

Today's Hells Angels, notes Len Isnor, are no longer
scruffy-looking, bearded Visigoths on Harleys—an image
out of popular films. They can be clean-cut, sophisticated
businessmen. "They wear their colours when they need to
wear their colours. The power of the patch. When they need
to show that they have the power, they wear those colours."

How then can the authorities beat them? "The government has to help us," says Isnor. And he means in the
courtrooms, where "procedures might be tied in knots" and
prosecutors must follow the law over what they can or can't
charge the HA with.

Isnor has lobbied fiercely to have the Hells Angels
scheduled as a criminal group, in the same way that drugs
such as cocaine and heroin are listed as illegal substances.
In 2002, a new federal anti-gang law was enacted that made
it an offence for a person to be knowingly associated with
a criminal organization, and such groups only need to have

three members. Sentences can be tougher, but the Crown still has had to prove each time that the Hells Angels *are* a criminal organization.

As an example of the frustrations police and prosecutors face, Isnor points to the trial in 2005 of two Hells Angels of the North Toronto Chapter, Stephen "Tiger" Lindsay and Raymond "Razor" Bonner.

Lindsay and Bonner got a satellite dish and a receiver for the bikers' clubhouse in Woodbridge from a dealer in black-market TVs, and they weren't happy when it turned out that the encryption codes on their equipment changed after a couple of weeks. They went back to the dealer, and not only did they want compensation, they also tried a severe shakedown. Wearing their Hell Angels colours when they met the man later at a restaurant, they demanded $75,000 and threatened him. The money, said Lindsay, belonged to him and "five other guys that are fucking the same kind of motherfucker as I am."

But the frightened dealer had gone to the cops, and Lindsay and Bonner were arrested after they left. "It took 10 days to prove the substantive, that they committed extortion—10 days of trial," Isnor points out. "Then five and a half months to prove that they're a criminal organization."

The trial, the hours invested by Crown prosecutors and police officers, was a huge expense for Canadian taxpayers, all "to prove water's wet" as far as Isnor is concerned.

"Why do we have to do this every time?…And we're doing it over and over and over again."

Nor are the courts always convinced, and it depends on where you live. Also in 2005, a BC Supreme Court judge decided that the anti-gang law was too broad and vague, and violated the Constitution, effectively quashing some charges that year against three BC Hells Angels. In 2009, again in BC, a provincial Supreme Court jury convicted four men of various charges of assault, extortion and weapons offences but acquitted them on the organization charges, basically saying that it wasn't a crime to be a Hells Angel.

Now consider the jurisdictional contradictions, the burden of proving the case of the Hells Angels being a criminal organization again and again, and remember, *there are more Hells Angels here than in any other country.* More than in the United States, which has the Racketeer Influenced and Corrupt Organizations Act, RICO as it's known—the federal law that nailed Mafia boss Frank Tieri and insider-trading financier Michael Milken.

"If we had RICO in this country, we wouldn't have the Hells Angels biker problem here," argues Isnor. "Why doesn't America have a biker problem? They have all kinds of bikers across the country. None of them is getting rich like the Canadian Hells Angels, because they have RICO.… That's why, in the United States, bikers are just bikers. They go out and do crazy things, but if they do anything really stupid, they're going away. So they're not really getting rich.

They're making a living, but they're not getting rich—like, the Hells Angels in Canada are millionaires. There's a number of them are millionaires because we created an environment here with our lax laws so these guys can do that. If we had RICO, ohhh, let me tell ya."

The Montréal police force's Deputy Chief Jacques Robinette says that as far as bikers are concerned in his city, cops haven't seen a patch since another major crackdown operation just before the summer of 2009. He doesn't doubt they're still around, but "They're laying very low—not low, *very* low. One thing that's helping police officers is the gangsterism law. Nobody's showing their face on the street since, like in bikers in Montréal, I would say, end of May, beginning of June...."

One last note about the criminal organizations issue and an interesting postscript to the Project Tandem investigation—in August 2009, the Hells Angels went to court to try to get their vests and insignia-bearing jewellery *back* from the police! But an Ontario Superior Court Justice, Gladys Pardu, ruled they were "offence-related property" that made it easier for the biker club members to commit crimes.

"The use of these items is intended to further the organizational purposes," she wrote. "It is used to intimidate and extort, and to serve as a badge of trustworthiness in the conduct of drug deals."

The bikers' lawyers had argued that all the goods belonged to the Hells Angels organization, *not* the individual members—so they should be given back. The judge didn't buy it—as far as she was concerned, that's like a gun maker asking for a weapon to be returned after it's been used in a crime.

The president of the Vancouver Hells Angels, Ricky Ciarniello, came out to testify that the HA doesn't condone lawbreaking. That still didn't wash with Justice Pardu. She pointed out that three-quarters of the club's members have criminal records.

So the very thing a club member prizes most—his vest with colours—wouldn't be handed back. Those confiscated vests and jewellery became the property of the federal government, and in a small but significant way, Canada took some of itself back from the Hells Angels.

Chapter Thirteen

The Way the Story's Told

This book is being written not only because gangs have become a problem in Canada but because gangs have become a public issue—one heavily covered by the media. So it's worth exploring just how well the media are explaining the problem.

People talk about the media as if it's a camera-wielding army, all walking in lockstep. But spend enough time in newsrooms, and you'll quickly discover there is no grand conspiracy over coverage of certain politicians or issues any more than there would be for gangs. If anything, what you often see is bias creeping in because, like anyone else, journalists are individuals who have their own opinions that can influence their work, and they do their jobs with varying degrees of professionalism. Some may not give a damn; others are brilliant. Consider the problems when reporters don't dig deeply enough or merely offer the so-called "broad strokes" because there is only so much time or space.

In 2009, for CTV's *W-Five*, distinguished reporter Paula Todd hit the streets of Regina to profile Aboriginal gangs. The show chose to consider the problem as "gangs" equals *"Aboriginal gangs"* in Regina. It did not choose to visit Vancouver, where gangs come in all shapes and sizes and where some of the worst violence, including machine-gun fire, has been happening. The report did not talk about Calgary, where, as we've seen, a bizarre feud is going on that has nothing to do with turf. It did not go to Winnipeg, where viewers might have seen Heather Robertson at work with young refugee kids at risk.

"Is the Native way of life violent?" Todd asked Kevin Daniels, the Interim National Chief of the Congress of Aboriginal Peoples.

You have to wonder what she expected Daniels to say—*Of course, it is*? A reporter's reflexive defence is that you ask such questions because you never know what some-one will answer. But here's a representative who will obvi-ously say that violence is not natural behaviour, and one suspects that this softball lob was a backend way for *W-Five* to avoid any accusations that it was demonizing the Aborig-inal community by exploring one of its uglier facets.

Todd goes down the usual checklist of addiction, poverty and unemployment to connect the dots to gang life, saying how "unemployment is high in the 'hood." (And if we can keep white, middle-class women from utilizing such slang, we will all cringe less.) But as others who study the problem have pointed out in these pages, there are scores of Native people who live in impoverished conditions, are jobless or have addiction issues who *don't* join gangs. It's just not that simple.

Daniels tells Todd how the "gang mentality" dates back to the 1990 Oka land dispute. This is how CTV puts it on its website: "He says Oka galvanized many young Aboriginals, but not in a positive way. 'These young people are looking to become warriors, but they've gone down a negative pathway to find that warrior image,' he said."

Oka, however, doesn't explain Jessie McKay playing gang enforcer on the streets of Winnipeg in the 1980s or the elders who told professor Kathy Buddle about how they fled residential schools to start some of the earliest gangs in the 1960s and '70s. Todd doesn't show anyone else offering a theory behind gang mentality, only Kevin Daniels' assertion of how gangs after Oka were more violent, with a negative warrior mentality. Daniels clarified his reasoning for *Gangs in Canada*, admitting the "criminal element was always there" for gangs pre-Oka, but "they weren't killing each other for nothing."

The segment claimed that Saskatchewan has become the province with the largest concentration of gang members. It asserted these two statements as if they were fact. The program's source didn't turn out to be a government or police authority, but an academic and consultant, Mark Totten. And if you check the actual paper that *W-Five* showed, it is entitled "Preventing Aboriginal Youth Gang Involvement in Canada: A Gendered Approach," which only cites earlier studies, some of them years old, and doesn't offer the methodology of how Totten came to single out Saskatchewan.

Given what's been happening recently in British Columbia and Alberta, Totten's assertion may be difficult to accept. It's also worth noting that *how* you count up the gang members makes a lot of difference. If you go by gang membership in correctional facilities, then you are factoring in individuals who had no choice and had to join for survival. Yes, you may say that a gang member in prison is still a member, but does what's happening in prisons reflect what is posing a long-term and current, ongoing threat out on the street?

If you go by self-identified gang members, do you include the bragging wannabes who claim to belong but may have only a loose affiliation? As one interview subject points out, she is considered a "gang affiliate" simply for communicating regularly with gang members—which happens to be part of her job. If you go by figures compiled by police authorities, then you have to ask how they add up their sums. It was also pointed out that cops might well inflate their figures as a political tool to gain more resources. Even if we give cops the benefit of the doubt, they will naturally go by incident reports, arrests and convictions, which certainly won't tell the whole story.

So this humble author thought it only fair to call Mark Totten up and ask him about all this. He confirmed that, yes, *W-Five* did check with him on his paper. And he informed me that his figures relied on a variety of sources—criminal intelligence divisions, correctional facilities and the like. I mentioned that it seemed to me that except for one citation to himself for 2008, most of his other cited sources for his figures were about five years old, and he admitted that the numbers were a "best guestimate" and that "we don't have any national data." But he stood by the claim that Saskatchewan has a higher rate of violent crime per capita than any other province. I pointed out that this isn't the same thing as suggesting that Saskatchewan has the highest proportion of gang members or that it's the hardest-hit province:

Me: "You were even cited as a gang expert on the program. Don't you think the situation is a little more complex than them zeroing in on Regina and the Native gang situation there?"

Totten: "I think you're missing the boat. You're focusing on one CTV *W-Five* episode, and you know, if I were you, I wouldn't be focussing my energy there. I would be looking at a variety of other sources across the country. But you do what you want, it's your book."

Me: "Oh, I am, sir, but the thing is, that's the impression they're giving to the general public in one report. They'll think 'gangs' equals 'Aboriginal gangs.'"

Totten: "But there are lots of other sources of data out there. So, I mean, yeah, there are problems with their report, but you know, with any other media report, too, there are problems, and what I would encourage you to do is forget about media as a source of official data, because the media doesn't do any science around it."

Now, to put things into context, I had called up Totten out of the blue. I explained that the book was a general survey of the gang situation in Canada, and that I had contacted him because I was exploring this one aspect, that of media coverage. My criticism, if any, was directed at CTV and wasn't an attack on his research. Since no one likes to be ambushed, and since perhaps he hadn't understood me, I explained *again* to him how I *wasn't* using the network for official data, I was merely commenting on the show's treatment of the subject. Then to be sure of his point, I asked him if he agreed with the show's contention that Aboriginal people made up most of the gang members in Saskatchewan.

"It doesn't do anybody any good just to make that statement," answered Totten, which is reasonable enough. "You've got to look at issues like the residential school system, colonization, land claims, all that kind of stuff."

"Well, that was my problem, sir," I said. "They didn't do that." I reminded him gently that they cited his paper as their source but didn't bother to speak to him on air or go into these more complex reasons for motivating youth into gangs.

When I asked Totten if he was happy with how they treated his material, he laughed and replied, "I'm indifferent. I don't have time to spend on it or to waste on it...."

But I pointed out that this is, after all, *his* issue, the one to which he has devoted a lot of his academic career, and this is how it's being covered and conveyed to the public.

"Is there anything else I can help you out with?" replied Totten curtly. "Because we're not going anywhere on this point."

I thanked him and hung up.

Keep in mind that this expert shapes important data that is taken on faith by one of our largest national media operations. And he says he is indifferent to what they do with it.

Oh, well. Not much help there. But back to the *W-Five* segment. In terms of community responses to the problem, reporter Paula Todd speaks on-air to a teacher and basketball coach and to another teacher who runs a theatre group. We get nice visuals of kids dancing. We get scary visuals of knives and what I presume must be bear spray displayed without any context. Where did the footage come from? Who are the kids in the shots?

For all his learn-as-you-go approach to journalism, filmmaker Mani Amar, a rank amateur, gets you to understand more about what makes gang life tick for the Punjabi community with a few talking heads in *A Warrior's Religion* than *W-Five* does with one high-profile reporter, two producers credited on-air and shots of kids dancing and of scary knives. Yes, Amar made a full-length documentary. He spoke to victims as well as gang members. He also bothered to get more than one opinion on the facets of the problem.

Why does all this matter? If the way we ask the questions frames the answers, the way we frame our stories affects opinions. In its attempt to always be seen as objective, mainstream journalism often puts forces into artificial opposition. A free press is fully entitled to demand from authorities what's being done about gangs. But sometimes stories are written in such an overwhelmingly negative fashion in the name of "balance" that all perspective is lost. It is not enough for a leading British newspaper to suggest that the sky is falling in Vancouver and that drug legalization is the way out of a war zone.

It's a cheap bit of theatre to end a report with language of hope, as *W-Five* does, contrasted against shots of knives and a police cruiser driving away, as if there were little hope at all and no one should sleep soundly in Regina. From professional experience, I am fairly sure what went through that video editor's head. He or she needed shots under Todd's voiceover. And he or she probably thought the visuals were "powerful"—never mind whether or not they said anything of substance.

Such reportage does have a direct effect on the very relationship the media has with the police. Since reporters are self-appointed critics on behalf of the public, police officers are often justifiably suspicious of how they will be portrayed and how their information will be reported.

I went back to the *Calgary Herald*'s Jason van Rassel for his opinion on how reporters are doing their jobs. Again and again, I had spoken to police officers who didn't want to identify specific gangs on the record, which begged the question of whether or not we're sensationalizing gang factions when we mention them. I wondered if such a policy was useless in the long run, since, yes, of course, reporters need to know who's doing what, and they'll inevitably find out.

Van Rassel got back to me by email and replied: "The police have their reasons for withholding gang names and, personally, I disagree with them—though I can appreciate their viewpoint and why they do it. It may suit their purposes, but our job in the media is to inform people, plain and simple. Withholding key factual information for some sort of ideological reason is not the role of the media. It's not serving our readers, and I think it's paternalistic to think that the public can't be trusted with the facts." He goes a step further in suggesting the public is *entitled* to the facts, especially when it comes to knowing who may be a threat to the community or to people's personal safety.

"It's convenient for police to look at the less-traditional gangs who self-identify and operate along more fluid lines and say, 'We're not going to identify them,' but think for a moment what would happen if the police applied that logic to easily identifiable criminal organizations like the Hells Angels," argues van Rassel. "And if the media went along with it. Without full and thorough reportage identifying the Hells Angels and detailing their criminal activities, we would be giving the HA free rein to keep perpetuating the myth that they're just a bunch of good ol' boys who like motorcycles."

I ran into a wall of resistance from some authorities across the country who saw little benefit in talking to me. Crown prosecutors in Ontario declined my invitation for interviews, even though I promised to withhold their names (a practice they insisted on during one major media event arranged by the authorities). Now *that* should bother you—*a lot*. I fully recognize that individuals are busy and have the priorities of their work, but when our institutions as a whole refuse to make themselves accountable to us, we have cause to worry. These prosecutors and police officers didn't want to explain themselves. They didn't want to tell a journalist, and therefore you, the public, how they are handling a major problem affecting our communities. They see a reporter as an antagonist, which means they do not fully trust the community they were hired to serve.

That should worry you a lot in a democracy.

But journalists can and should do their jobs better. I was interested to know how van Rassel would rate our profession in covering gangs. Were we contributing to a climate of fear or actually enlightening folks on the issue? He agreed that was a valid question—and in his own view, the media does a poor job of covering crime in general, and day-to-day coverage often lacks needed context and statistics.

"There are several investigative journalists in Canada (Julian Sher, Michel Auger, Kim Bolan) who have done an outstanding service to the public by exposing the extent of the threat that organized crime and gangs pose to society," van Rassel wrote back. "But I think the media falls down on the daily stuff, which tends to be too shallow and simplistic—and the danger there is that those are the stories most people see. The people who take the time to read books and/or multi-part investigative news series are in the minority."

He cites the example of how, at least in Calgary, many media outlets—particularly TV—will say, "it's not known if it's gang-related." For van Rassel, that carries the unspoken—and utterly erroneous—assumption that the only people carrying guns and using them are gang members. "Not every incidence of unexplained/unsolved gunfire should be viewed through the prism of gang violence! People get shot in domestic disputes, to name just one of a multitude of other possible scenarios."

Another one of his pet peeves, he says, came from a local TV station when it ran a logo in the background whenever it reported on a gang story. Written in spray-paint style letters on a brick wall, it read something like "GANG WAR" or "GANGS OF CALGARY."

"It looked like something out of *West Side Story*," complains van Rassel, "but had absolutely nothing to do with the reality of gangs in Calgary, which have never had a history or culture of using graffiti to 'tag' geographic territory."

The way we ask our questions. The way we frame our stories. They affect our opinions. So the media, too, can do better when it comes to the gang issue.

Chapter Fourteen

Complaints Against Culture: A Personal View

I t's only fair to warn you that in a book of stories, this next one never happened. You're certainly entitled to know this, since this book will go on the shelves for *non-fiction*—and I promise you I'm going somewhere with this. Imagine this gang. At this point, no made-up one could be as viciously demoralizing and soulless as some of those we've met, but come along with me on a brief trip…

≈

The cold is better, Cal decided, pushing his hands into the pockets of his leather jacket as they strolled along. Fucking cold wakes you up. In the apartment, he'd been falling asleep after hours of playing *Batman Arkham Asylum* on his Xbox, and there was nothing to do since he'd done collections, and the guys wanted to party. Restless, he didn't bother to put on his toque and left his shaved head to feel the chill. Feel fucking *something.* He hadn't felt anything since noon when Suze turned up late, and he couldn't have that, guys would call him a little bitch for letting her get away with that shit, so he gave her a shot in the belly where it wouldn't show and ripped her crappy clothes to give her a scare, but he got excited over that and took her rough in the building hall with the cracked, peeling paint. She cried. Like that should make him stop. Go make some money, slut, he told her. When that didn't move her ass, he talked sweet to her.

Cal was good at talking. When he was back in school before he quit for good, the teacher said his English papers showed potential, and he had an instinct for clever phrases. He made Danny and Sunil laugh their asses off when they sat on a curb, and Danny complained about some stupid Jehovah's Witness actually coming to his mom's door. "Yeah, they say the meek shall inherit the Earth," sneered Cal. "The minute they do, we'll fucking rip it right back from them!" And then he turned his head and spat.

Tonight, he was sick of all the shit. Same thing, every night, and they weren't moving up, and the guys weren't listening to him about the hook-up with the Killerz he just *knew* would make them lots of money. He bummed a smoke off Danny, always looking so friggin' scared by him with those wide eyes in that freckled face, so scared that he could always take Danny's smokes. He felt adrenaline pumping, needing a release.

When he saw the couple, guy and girl their age, walk-ing the opposite side of the street, he hated them on sight. The guy was tall, mixed race, lanky. The girl was blonde, white, fantastic curves. The kind of chick who wouldn't get on her back for Cal unless he got her using. Guy was carry-ing a gym bag.

"Hey!" called Cal. Then harder, angrier, "*HEY!*"

Because he hated this smug tree of a kid who proba-bly went to a fucking gym all the time and had his snotty ho, and because you just *take* the money off 'em, and he wasn't going to spend the rest of his life bagging takes from whores like Suze every goddamn afternoon. The guys ought to see. The guys have to *know*.

Cal barked at the guy to give him his money, pulling out his knife, and now his crew was loping up like wolf cubs, only something hardened in the guy's eyes, like he knew they would stab him and beat the shit out of him any-way, wallet or no, and take the girl somewhere. Which is exactly what Cal intended.

The moment took forever.

It took all of two seconds.

The young man's name was Sean, not that Cal would ever know that, because Sean's answer was to bring up his foot in a cobra-snap forward, the kick slamming his attacker in the belly like a battering ram. Like a building demolition, Cal collapsed, cement slapping his face, not knowing that three of his ribs had been snapped. He tried to breathe, and pain *expanded* through his chest, pain and rolling pain.

Sean and the girl turned and ran.

"You did *exactly* the right thing," Sean's teacher told him the next day. "You didn't stick around for heroics. You got your girlfriend safe. That's what counts."

Sean smiled faintly and bowed. He tightened the black belt around his waist and then jogged back onto the mat, where a line of young men and women his own age were punching and kicking in time to numbers in Japanese. "*Ichi! Ni! San! Shi! Go…*"

∼

There are certain familiar movie ingredients in the scenario above. By focusing on our teenage sociopath, we're forced to identify with him, whether we want to or not. I gave him the "cool" line, as is so typical with villains these days (I actually stole it from a certain former TV producer known infamously in the business as a major jerk and who said this "meek shall inherit" line *all* the time). I hint at what could be a major story arc by referring to Cal's ambition…until I quite deliberately, arbitrarily manipulate the reader's point of view to an actual hero in the story. Heroes aren't supposed to get their asses kicked, so now we know who we *should* root for. There are reasons why I made you follow Cal, and why I switched over to Sean. I'll get to them.

You see, I've waited for certain things to be said about culture and gangs, and I'm still waiting, so I will have to write them here myself. I looked in vain for them from gang expert Michael Chettleburgh's book, *Young Thugs*, but he points out a lot of the obvious, asking rather pointlessly, "Should we ban video games?" (when he knows we can't) and affecting a nice, safe liberal view that rap is really a complex art form, when *anything* can be a complex art form in the hands of the talented—but not everyone is. My main quibble with Mr. Chettleburgh, despite all the reviewer praise that fills a page of his paperback edition, is that he is not thinking "deep thoughts." He'd rather dismiss the question of culture altogether and get back to socio-economic causes, which is not good enough.

When it comes to culture, you can be left with the impression that there are only two sides to the issue: you either believe that video games, music and movies cause violence, or you believe the academics who point out there is no causal link. To suggest that a gory movie prompts teens to go out and commit violence is overly simplistic, but it is equally unfair to casually dismiss those who are appalled by the nihilism they see expressed in our media products.

Constable Garrett Swihart of the Calgary police force, for instance, cites a commercial that he says "gets him riled every once in a while." In the spot, Lee Iacocca, the former CEO of Chrysler, is paired with Snoop Dogg, the rap star who was once a member of the notorious Crips. In the commercial, Iacocca seemingly admires Mr. Calvin "Snoop" Broadus, for whom women, at least in his creative work, are "bitches" and "hos."

"I've got kids who want to stand up and do the Crip walk in the school when I ask who do they know that's a gangster?" says Swihart. "And they want to show me Snoop Dogg's Crip walk. And it's like, 'Oh ho, I don't want to see that!' Because you know what that dance is. And they don't! They don't know that that dance is about him wiping the blood off his shoes from a Blood that he just killed."

Nor can you easily dismiss the concern of Acting Staff Sergeant Gordon Eiriksson of the Calgary police about *Grand Theft Auto*, "where it's perfectly acceptable to kill a police officer, to decapitate a prostitute and urinate on her body. And steal a car and drive away. *That's* how you win the game. So what are we teaching the kids when it comes to these things?"

What, indeed? We have to keep in mind, though, that our art forms have never been accurate mirrors of society. They have always been windows, looking out on the various ripples in the ocean of the popular mindset, as well as the choppy waves of what we will tolerate. The "anti-hero" phase in movies during the 1970s allowed room for future portrayals of morally ambiguous heroes and just plain "anti-people"—characters with no redeeming virtues. This is why we have *Grand Theft Auto*, in which the avatar can decapitate a prostitute. It is the anti-hero extended to its logical conclusion where there is no more "hero," only a sociopathic nihilist like the fictional Cal with whom I started the chapter.

When Garrett Swihart ran into young men sporting *Scarface* belt buckles and Tony Montana shirts, they were, of course, already gang members. Al Pacino certainly didn't make them go out and commit crimes. What they got out of these affectations was the reinforcement of a myth they have to tell themselves to justify their existence. *I will wear Scarface, which suggests I'm like Scarface*—I'm not a punk who actually leads a pretty shitty life with odds of ending up in jail, the morgue or a hospital bed. This is the lie I will tell myself.

On the other side of the country, Detective Sergeant Len Isnor of the Biker Enforcement Unit says, "I can't tell you how many search and seizures I've conducted where I've found *Scarface* on the wall."

In my personal DVD collection, I have a copy of *Scarface*—the 1932 version. That's right, when you watch Al Pacino, you're watching a remake. It's a genuine classic, but it's also *really* violent—there is a bombing, a man gunned down as he lays in his hospital bed, about *eight* drive-by shootings, at least seven of them with machine guns drilling both the walls and people, and a re-enactment of the Saint Valentine's Day Massacre.

Yet no one can claim gangster movies back then made young men run out and pick up automatics to go knock off banks—and remember, there were scores of films with Bogart, Edward G. Robinson, James Cagney and George Raft. Truth be told, the original *Scarface* doesn't have a moral message that is superior to the Pacino version, but it does have something to say about the human condition—and it's just better art.

Nor do we want or need to banish anti-heroes forever from our books and narratives. As this book comes out, we'll soon see a remake of a 1979 cult film, so aptly titled *The Warriors*. It will be interesting to see if it preserves the actual point of the story. In the film, a typical gang of hoodlums, the Warriors, is blamed for another gangster's death in a New York park and must fight their way back to their home turf of Coney Island. It's based on a novel that was actually inspired by Xenophon's *Anabasis*.

Much of it is B-movie violence, but there are several scenes that lift it to greatness. One of them is this: after all the battles, the gang manages to hop on a subway train for a final leg home in the small hours of the morning. They've had it— dishevelled, bloody and bruised, members lost. The doors open at a station, and a laughing group of kids in prom formal wear gets on, completely oblivious at first to who is sitting across from them. The two groups eye each other warily, knowing exactly by contrast what they each have and *don't* have. The tag-along girl in the Warriors tries to fix her mussed hair, and the default hero, Swan, takes her hand, prompting her to stop fidgeting and keep some dignity.

Just before this moment, one tired Warrior says to the others, "It's all out there. All we got to do is figure out a way to go steal it."

"Sounds great," snaps another, who's had enough. "All you got to do is figure out what's worth stealing."

~

Our movies as well as our music, TV and video games only fail young people because we have already failed in a more crucial sales job with our culture, the one selling them the wrong product. In many cases, with our stories and songs, we've told them the wrong things to earn, let alone steal.

Consider one of the "cure alls" often suggested for gangs: sports. Now, socialization through group activity has merit. But we also sell kids and teens the idea that if you are a fabulous athlete, a university scholarship will be handed to you on a plate, as well as Olympic medals, fame and your face on a cereal box. Except that most of us will never make it to the NHL or the NBA. Our athlete worship is merely another facet of the celebrity-obsessed *Entertainment Tonight* coverage that relentlessly bombards our young people.

What athletes do is often the pursuit of *individual* glory. All of us, not just young people, so rarely see our scientist heroes deified, our superstars of biology, chemistry, medicine who contribute something of value to *everyone*, not just themselves. Worse, there are often no role models celebrated in these positions for *minority* youth. The message is reinforced time and again that your ticket out of a deprived life comes mainly through a basketball hoop or a hip-hop track.

If our celebrity-obsessed culture offers the false promise that fame equals privilege and living outside the rules, at the opposite end of the spectrum, we have the warped idea that poverty and criminal experience equals wisdom. We are talking here about "street cred." It's not a new idea. Bertrand Russell wrote an essay on the fallacy of the superior virtue of the oppressed. But Compton rap tunes in the 1980s and '90s suggested life was somehow more "authentic" because of the inherent danger and meanness of poverty in the 'hood. The truth is that poverty doesn't ennoble anyone—it's just dull and desperate and soul killing—while children who witness violence are sure to incur psychological damage.

It's interesting, as someone pointed out to me, that so many ex-gang members seek out the spotlight by trying to be a rap performer or gang-awareness speaker. Rap is a democratic genre. You don't actually need to read music or even have singing talent to dabble, but again, these ex-gang members believe experience of violence equals legitimacy. Yes, there is value in an ex-gang member telling kids to avoid the life because they know its perils. Yet the success of their example is primarily shown in *leaving*. They tell kids, "You must go out and work," but their "work" rests on their credibility as having lived a life of violence and never having experienced nine-to-five even once—at least not before their public disavowal of their old ways. What do they truly know about ordinary life and the sweet accomplishments of stability and family, which is what we're *really* hoping to sell our young people?

Gang life is sometimes an option, and many times it's conscription onto a path of anarchy. If you want young people to critically reject anarchy, you'd better do a superb job of heralding the virtues of peace and order. Toronto Staff Sergeant Sharon Davis called gangs a social issue, and she is right. If a gang member robs someone, it's because he believes theft is easier than working. The problem with the "hard work" message is that we have failed to sell young people on what we should be working so hard for.

We don't tell them in our music and our movies that the world is full of joys and wonders to be found in the work of a microbiologist or a geological engineer or a museum curator. We have narrowed the glory to a few select creative fields and sports, and then promised them with our silence that if you choose the rest, you will be another drone in the hive. As they cross into their teens, we tell them that knowledge must have a vocational purpose instead of being a pursuit they can follow recreationally for the rest of their lives. No wonder we have so much escapist entertainment that celebrates anarchy and nihilism.

Faced with the drudgery of work and the crystallizing truth that fame is a lottery and that they'll never be rock stars or movie legends, it's not difficult either to see why so many young people, especially young men, seek out the identity of the *warrior*. It's an idyll that's at least accessible because they're mostly inventing it as they go. The warrior supposedly lives by a code (though it might be a code these youths created themselves a couple of weeks ago). The warrior is larger than life, certainly larger than that sad, anonymous hard worker who in many cases has to run to stand still. The pity is that these gangsters are groping their way unconsciously towards an idyll that already has a developed precedent: martial arts.

It's a ridiculous misconception that the martial arts promote violence. The paradox of training in arts such as aikido, karate, tai chi and others is that as you learn to defend yourself, you are sculpting and polishing your character, making you lose interest in causing anyone harm. A martial art does, indeed, offer a culture—unique clothes (the training *gi* and belts), a specific language of technical terms and etiquette, and its own history of founders and great teachers. In karate and aikido, the word for instructor is *sensei*, which does not mean "he who walks on water" or even "teacher"—it means "he who has gone before." Respect for experience is the guiding principle. At the dojo where I trained, there were black belts of all ethnicities and professions. Among others, there was a garbage man, the part owner of a restaurant and a jet aircraft mechanic. At one point, it had a Filipino Catholic priest. It is a place for camaraderie, the genuine article, with young men and women who are mindful of safety and who won't turn on each other at the drop of a hat. They have something to offer young gang recruits, staggering through a back alley of pain and self-loathing, desperate to define themselves.

As a character-building education, however, these arts rely on a student to persevere, eventually becoming enlightened. Even my sensei conceded, "Martial arts aren't for everybody." The will and the investment of effort must still come largely from the individual. An apparently exotic, mysterious Asian discipline might strike a note with one young person and be complete noise to another. So what else can we offer as more preventative measures with our culture? A lot, actually. We can start by changing our way of thinking about it and being more responsible in our choices.

I have written and sold novels, and I know people vote with their wallets over what to read or watch. We can monitor what our children and teenagers read and buy, and we can turn off the lewd 50 Cent music video. We don't have to bring home the DVD release of *Saw XXV*, or whatever number the series is up to. We can insist our children spend an hour listening to jazz or classical music—other genres of music they can learn to appreciate. We can insist they read a *book* in the living room. Every day, not just once in a while. One that tells a compelling story or opens their eyes to nature, history, art—substance.

As much as this book has touched sometimes on economic deprivation, and others want to ascribe gang ills mostly to this, this country does have public libraries. They cost you next to nothing except for late fees. This country does have public radio. Few are so poor that they do not have a TV set over which they can exercise choices. It is a matter of will, of taking ownership and responsibility.

We can do more in remembering that culture includes social behaviour. While it may sound quaint, we can insist our offspring call an older person "sir" or "ma'am." One of the things my karate sensei used to bemoan was the loss of manners, because in manners were rituals that gave people clues to how being civilized ought to work. It is no accident that children who address an adult casually as an equal have a harder time deferring to an older person's experience.

When we talk about being overwhelmed by media, we forget that we shape the tastes of our children even when we don't raise a hand to switch off a TV set or turn down the volume. Leave them to their own devices and, yes, you likely will not know what they are learning. But you can always seek out the good, the educational, the uplifting, which frankly means you discriminate in your selections as well. You can watch *Nova* on PBS for one night instead of another episode of *So You Think You Can Dance*. You can have your children learn a foreign language for one hour instead of playing a video game for three. It is the same as the choice between Pringles for dinner or vegetable stir-fry. There's a diet for building character as well as bodies. Feed their minds.

Chapter Fifteen

Postscript: A Chance for a Normal Life

This book, unfortunately, doesn't have a real ending. The busts and arrests go on, the gang feuds keep sparking fresh violence. As *Gangs in Canada* was completed, life sentences with no chance of parole were handed down for the killers of eight Toronto-area Bandidos, members of the "No Surrender Crew," found shot to death on a quiet road near Shedden back in 2006. Vancouver police were investigating a gangland shooting off Cambie Village that killed one man in his 30s. And in Winnipeg in late September 2009, police launched Project Restore, a new anti-gang initiative in which they aggressively enforced bail and probation conditions for top gang members and high-risk offenders.

While details of Project Restore were leaked to the media ahead of its announcement, Jessie McKay was setting up a new life away from Winnipeg. As mentioned earlier, McKay—the female gang member known as "Big Jess" who reinvented herself as a crisis intervention worker and program coach—moved west to become an outreach worker for Regina Anti-Gang Services. But as much as McKay likes her new job, it turns out she and her partner had to get out of Winnipeg fast. And it's because the old life won't leave her man alone. For safety reasons, his name won't be used here.

Once upon a time, he was a prospect for the Bandidos in Manitoba, and he was apparently quite skilled at selling drugs for the motorcycle club in a certain town. He was caught and went to prison over drug offences, served his time, and although he went back for a spell in 2008 for breaching probation conditions, McKay says that after his release, her man kept out of trouble for months. He's been trying to start a new life as an auto mechanic. But she says since 2006, old acquaintances have been bugging him to get back into gang life. They don't like giving up on such talent.

The threat, says McKay, now comes from Rock Machine, and in the ever-shifting world of biker gang allegiances, with the Bandidos recently on the wane in Canada, 10 full-patch members who were left at loose ends actually went the reverse path—patching over to Rock Machine, the gang that had patched over to the Bandidos in eastern Canada during the biker war. McKay says that a high-ranking

Winnipeg Bandidos member, currently in an Edmonton prison, has been pulling strings, pushing for her partner's re-enlistment with a steady campaign of harassment. It involves everything from a barrage of phone calls and cell texts to showing up unexpectedly at their house. Just do this for us, we need you to drop this off, you got to go do this for us, man. The basic message, says McKay, is clear: we consider you in until you die.

McKay says her man approached the Winnipeg police for help, but the cops wanted him to commit to working as an informant for them. When he refused, not wanting to get in any deeper (and incur further risk to himself, McKay and those he cares for), she says they told him bluntly, "You're on your own. If something happens, call 911."

McKay says no death threats were made, but she fully expected the harassment to escalate to violence, and she and her partner weren't about to stick around to find out if it did. It's true that some gang members "age out" and can escape the life. But then there's the cautionary tale of Jessie McKay and her man, still trying to escape gang life even after they've left it.

He isn't really known to the biker clubs in Regina. But then, people can always pick up a phone and pass the word around over his past and who he is.

"I have no idea how this is going to go down," says McKay, "and you know what? Right now, I'm just kind of sitting on the edge of a chair. I don't know. He doesn't, either."

McKay says they just want a normal life now that they're away from Winnipeg. "To hold down some jobs, you know, pay some bills—not have to look over our shoulders all the time."

Jeff Pearce began his writing and journalism career over 25 years ago when he sold his first article to the *Winnipeg Sun*. A journalism graduate from the Creative Communications program at Red River Community College, Jeff has worked as a writer and editor for TV and magazines, both in Canada and the UK. In 2005, he taught journalism on a short-term contract in Myanmar (Burma), a country where reporters are routinely harassed and often imprisoned. His eight novels, published under pseudonyms in the UK and the U.S., have won several awards, while his play, *Defenders of Gravity*, inaugurated the Playwrights of Spring Festival in Toronto. Currently, Jeff is a freelance writer and is working on a variety of non-fiction projects.

Check out more True Crime from
QUAGMIRE PRESS

Available April 2010

CANADIAN CON ARTISTS
by Lisa Wojna

Con artists everywhere exploit human virtues—trust, hope, compassion—and twist them into weaknesses, all in the hopes of making a quick buck. From cons who misrepresent and misguide to those who just downright lie, read about some of Canada's most convincing con men.

$18.95 • ISBN: 978-1-926695-06-8 • 5.25" x 8.25" • 256 pages

FALLEN OFFICERS
Canadian Police in the Line of Fire
by Peter Boer

Canadian police officers put their lives on the line every day in order to preserve a lawful society. Sadly, they sometimes pay the ultimate price. Fallen Officers is a memorial to the men and women whose sacrifices deserve to be remembered and whose heroic stories need to be told.

$18.95 • ISBN: 978-0-9783409-4-0 • 5.25" x 8.25" • 256 pages

DEADLY CANADIAN WOMEN
The Stories Behind the Crimes of Canada's Most Notorious Women
by Patricia MacQuarrie

Some Canadian women have done the unthinkable and murdered spouses, lovers, children, even complete strangers. These women are from across Canada and across social backgrounds, and many of their cases have changed the Canadian criminal justice system. This book tells their stories.

$18.95 • ISBN: 978-0-9783409-2-6 • 5.25" x 8.25" • 256 pages

UNSOLVED MURDERS OF CANADA
by Lisa Wojna

The murder of someone you know and love is tragic enough. More so if the murder remains unsolved. This book puts the spotlight on a number of killings for which the perpetrators have yet to be brought to justice.

$18.95 • ISBN: 978-0-9783409-5-7 • 5.25" x 8.25" • 256 pages

Available from your local bookseller or by contacting the distributor,

Lone Pine Publishing

1-800-661-9017

www.lonepinepublishing.com